“Suffering is the fear-laden, painful anticipation of the past,” writes Swiss psychotherapist J. Konrad Stettbacher in this ground-breaking book. Suffering is the result of primal wounding of a child before he can understand abuse, articulate his pain and outrage, or bear the pain of being unloved and uncared for. Because a child’s system is not capable of handling or processing the ideas of rejection and abuse, he or she represses the memory, which lingers on to affect negatively his or her ability to function as an adult while striving to avoid the pain of the past. And traditional psychotherapeutic and analytic techniques offer no help in accessing and resolving this repressed pain. In this thoughtful work, Stettbacher provides the theoretical framework for his primal therapy, and then gives systematic, detailed information about his revolutionary four-step program for helping an adult to become the caring, conscious advocate of the once hurt inner child. He offers advice on proceeding for people who wish to find the path to their own life history, step by step, with the help of this method.

J. KONRAD STETTBACHER is a Swiss psychotherapist. Since 1972, he has been in private practice, using the primal therapy that he developed. He lives in Switzerland.

MAKING SENSE OF SUFFERING

The healing confrontation with your own past

J. Konrad Stettbacher

Originally published in German under the name
Wenn Leiden einen Sinn haben Soll.

Translated by Simon Worrall

A MERIDIAN BOOK

MERIDIAN
Published by the Penguin Group
Penguin Books USA Inc., 375 Hudson Street, New York, New York 10014, U.S.A.
Penguin Books Ltd, 27 Wrights Lane, London W8 5TZ, England
Penguin Books Australia Ltd, Ringwood, Victoria, Australia
Penguin Books Canada Ltd, 10 Alcorn Avenue, Toronto, Ontario, Canada M4V 3B2
Penguin Books (N.Z.) Ltd, 182–190 Wairau Road, Auckland 10, New Zealand

Penguin Books Ltd, Registered Offices: Harmondsworth, Middlesex, England

First published by Meridian, an imprint of Dutton Signet, a division of Penguin Books USA Inc. Previously published in a Dutton edition.

First Meridian Printing, October, 1993
10 9 8

Originally published in Germany as *Wenn Leiden einen Sinn haben Soll* by Hoffmann and Campe Verlag. © 1990 by Hoffmann and Campe Verlag, Hamburg.

 REGISTERED TRADEMARK—MARCA REGISTRADA

LIBRARY OF CONGRESS CATALOGING IN PUBLICATION DATA:

Stettbacher, J. Konrad, 1930-
[Wenn Leiden einen Sinn haben soll. English]
Making sense of suffering : the healing confrontation with your own past / J. Konrad Stettbacher; translated by Simon Worrall.
p. cm.
Originally published: New York : Dutton, 1991
Includes bibliographical references and index.
ISBN 0-452-01159-0
1. Primal therapy. 2. Inner child. I. Title.
[RC489.P67S7413 1993]
616.89'14—dc20 93-8157
CIP

Printed in the United States of America
Original hardcover designed by Leonard Telesca

Making sense of suffering means resolving it. To do so, I believe, we have to seek and determine its causes today in order to prevent its recurring tomorrow.

Contents

MAKING SENSE OF SUFFERING

Introduction

Life can be a joyful, peaceful experience. Our actions can be guided by supportiveness, creativity, and understanding. Anyone who has experienced this truth, for even a short time, would inevitably wish to do everything in their power to maintain and preserve the gift of life.

Evidently we have not yet arrived at that point. Destructiveness threatens us and the entire planet. By virtue of his learning abilities, his reproductive capabilities, and his social nature, man has become the undisputed "Lord of Creation." At the same time, because of the way we treat other forms of life, we pose the greatest threat to life on earth. This fact alone should prompt us to reassess our relationship to nature and our fellow human beings and lead us toward change. Our destructiveness must have causes. By discovering them, we can rectify the wrong.

Our lives are in our own hands. As adults each of us is responsible for our actions and must accept their consequences. If we are not prompted to act badly, our actions will be guided by reason and good sense.

Why do we, in fact, find it so difficult to live creatively? The conditions for fulfillment exist. All we have to do is respect and satisfy our natural needs. So long as these remain natural, so long as our primal needs have not been deformed, they are not insatiable.

Or are certain species doomed to extinction? Do we have to go on increasing our population until the imbalance of nature, the depletion of food supplies, and overconsumption drive us to extinction? Or is it a particularly "human" form of aggression, an innate destructiveness, increasing in direct proportion to the ever-declining quality of our lives, that is propelling us toward destruction? Is it a legacy of the past, a compulsion to annihilate everything that threatens us, even if it is our fellow creatures?

These are all possible secondary causes. *The crisis of mankind, however, stems from our incomplete and disrupted consciousness. Each of us must realize that we are dependent on one another and dependent upon the environment and that the environment responds to all our actions.* As soon as we lose the ability to feel and understand without fear, we are in danger. For it is fear, of each other and of the environment, that prevents us from arriving at clear, life-enhancing decisions and acting constructively. Our unconscious fear that we are deficient, that we are worthless or "bad"—*this* is the root of all our negative compensations and developments. A person whose primal nature has received support and confirmation will take pleasure in being alive and will not act destructively.

Fear, as it appears in the myths and sagas of mankind's infancy or the various symbolic attempts to elucidate man's dilemma, should really be a thing of the past. We know the history of our race and its evolution. We *can* explain the origins of the universe and its different forms of life. But as long as parents continue to burden their children with moral tales that inspire fear in them and distort the truth, this source of fear remains very much alive.

Unconscious fear born of the anxieties and pain experienced in childhood, coupled with guilt feelings, produces what I shall call an overload of consciousness. This in turn gives rise to many kinds of distorted attitudes that affect our ability to communicate and to act. The result is suffering and the impairment of our sense of well-being.

Fear derives from primal "overloads." Its consequence is invariably suffering. That suffering is not confined to the individual alone, however. It can also lead to economic and, not least, ecological problems. Because suffering leads to fear and confusion and limits our capacity to anticipate future realities with wisdom, the world we inhabit will inevitably become sicker and sicker. Misjudgment and faulty decisions lead to defective action. This in turn creates unconscious feelings of guilt that sow the seeds of future misjudgments. This is the vicious circle set in motion by what I shall call "psychic suffering."

In order to avoid psychic suffering in the future, we must first understand what it is and how it arises. Suffering is the manifestation of our being ill, weak, and bowed down, of our being consumed by need and crippled. It is the refrain of our distress and pain, the dirge of our fears and despair. It is what we are feeling when we say we are "close to the brink." In fact, psychic suffering appears to be *the* source of suffering per se. All the more reason for us to face the questions: what is psychic suffering? how does it arise?

What Is Psychic Illness?

The German term for the soul—*Seele*—derives from the word *See,* meaning "lake" or "ocean." Originally, *soul* meant "that which belongs to the lake." According to ancient tradition, the unborn and the dead dwelt in the water.

The soul—or psyche—is that which constitutes our powers of sensing, feeling, and thought, the entirety of our experiences and all our memories.

In the human organism, the soul has no habitat as such. The sum of a person's memories, including his or her racial memories, is necessary to the successful survival of each member of the species. The outward manifestation of the soul is the sum of everything that we say and do. Or, to put it another way: Our soul is the outward expression of that which moves us, raising it to the surface for the maintenance and defense of life.

If our ability to maintain life has been impaired or misdirected, we are endangered or will become ill, be it as an individual, a member of a group, or a social being. To be "psychically ill" means that our system of self-survival has been damaged.

The question is: why and how does such impairment to our "system" occur?

The word *system* signifies an "integrated whole." A human being, as created by nature and born into the world, is such a system—an exceptionally complex, marvelous, perfectly functioning whole that is both self-sufficient and in dialogue with the outside world. Its purpose is to ensure the maintenance of the species.

Because it is, in its primal stage, weak and dependent, this system requires the selfless devotion and help of its progenitors and relatives for its survival.

To be able to perceive and satisfy its needs, a child's progenitors must establish an affirmative, responsible, and caring relationship to it. If the child's natural, primal needs are satisfied, it will be endowed with a fundamental feeling of security, trust, and vitality. Together these will form the foundation for a positive ability to form human attachments. If these requirements are met, the human "system" will be optimally endowed with the ability to enter into relationships and live and love in the fullest sense. To fulfill these conditions, we have to know what the child needs. The infant human being clearly signals these needs, and every mother recognizes them instinctively. Her willingness to respond to them is crucial to the child. A child needs a great deal of attention. It needs optimal nutrition, caring, devoted attention and calm people around it who encourage it with their love. In other words, it needs an environment that protects it and allows it to test and discover itself. It also needs appropriate information and insights to ground it in reality. The developing human being needs all these things to enable it to establish and maintain a positive, confident relationship to itself and its environment.

When those *primal needs* are not met, a child will become unsure of itself. If its tears or calls for help go unheeded, it will increasingly become a helpless prey to fear and pain. Unfortunately, the child will interpret this as a product of *its own* inadequacy. To realize that it is being neglected in the moment of its need is for the child insupportable. If the situation then continues, the child will, out of self-defense, become nonfeeling and nonsensing. Otherwise, it would suffer physical harm or even die. The child will notice that something is wrong with its self-preservation system. But because its appeals to its environment go entirely or partially unheeded, because no help is forthcoming, its ability to form relationships will become increasingly impaired. Ultimately, it will become disturbed.

Unfulfilled needs lead to the impairment of our ability to form relationships.

Impairment at the individual level will also lead to dysfunction at the wider, social level. The extent to which this will make itself negatively felt will depend on the strength and receptivity of the larger system.

In my definition of "psychic illness," I contend that it is a disturbance of our ability to relate to others caused by people who are themselves disturbed. This is, I admit, a blunt and unsettling assertion. Probably *everyone* will feel himself "implicated" and go on the defensive. No one wants to bear the guilt of causing others to suffer. We often suffer, if not chronically, from our inability to relate to ourselves or those around us. We suffer because of circumstances or things that we do not want to perceive because we do not comprehend why we are suffering. Even when we are at the end of our rope, we prefer to hide our weakness. Thus, the first step to solving our problems in relating is to acknowledge that they exist. To do this we have to be willing to call into question both ourselves and the entire collective in order to discover the causes of our disturbed consciousness. Only thus will we be able to make the necessary changes to our way of relating and to our behavior.

In turn, this means that "psychic illness" and "disturbance" cannot be healed from outside ourselves. We must each personally want that change, make the necessary decisions to bring it about, and act on them.

It is fair to assume that the human organism, "the system," if it is protected by a healthy, supportive environment, is in harmony with itself (self-congruent) at a given time before or after birth. The three faculties by which we relate to the world, the compass points of the soul, so to speak—sensing (bodily); feeling (emotional); thinking (reason)—are still intact and functioning. If no hereditary diseases or genetic deformations are present, if we are of sound constitution and our environment is supportive, we have to then ask ourselves: how is it that psychic disturbances can occur?

Psychic disturbances manifest themselves as defective reactions toward the outside world or ourselves. They are reactions that confuse, inhibit, endanger, or damage us as individuals or the community.

In my opinion, it is the fact of our being injured or intact (our integrity) and the degree to which our "system" is self-congruent that determines our reactions, inasmuch as these are outward manifestations of the soul. An overload (trauma) results in damage to the child's primal self-congruence and its ability to order experience. The injury is caused by fear and

pain-eliciting stimuli to which the young organism can only react incompletely, if at all, and which it cannot adequately integrate into its system.

Overloads are pains and anxieties for which there appear to be no causes or whose causes cannot or, in the interests of self-preservation, may not, be realized. These overloads (traumas) aggravate the system, disturbing primal functionality and integrity.

Far-reaching psychic injuries originate in deformations of personal (ontogenetic) and historic (phylogenetic) truths or in the distortion of reality. Such injuries to a person's cognitive integrity—for example, through unreal religious doctrines—can result in profound insecurities within the system.

The resultant psychic traumas cause confusion to the entire system. Many real experiences that should serve to develop consciousness must thereby be banished to the unconscious because they cannot be made to correspond with the received, unreal versions of reality.

All injuries to and overloads of the infant human being's primal integrity arise from the negation of its needs. Neglect, disregard, and unreasonable demands—combined with the recurrent experience of receiving too little good, and too much bad, treatment—will overload and disturb the young person's system. Usually this is not done intentionally. It is simply passed on blindly from generation to generation.

In the traumatized system, a multiplicity of unconscious, latent reactions, directed both outward and inward, become vehicles for the symptoms we characterize as neurosis, psychosomatic ailments, criminal behavior, or psychosis. All of these "aberrations" can be grouped under the heading psychic illness.

To be psychically ill is therefore to have been injured in one's primal integrity, to be a person whose original self-congruence has been traumatized. In such a person the ability to live consciously and function fully is impaired.

How do injures arise? What are their consequences?

At the beginning of its life, a human being is, so to speak, all body. Our perceptions and the resultant reactions are governed by the senses. These signal heat and cold, softness and hardness, loud and soft, bright and dark. Good and bad are still synonymous with pain and pleasure. Words are still unknown. *Sensing—the first level of perception*—is the only language we know. We are "pure sensation." Already in the womb these sense experiences give rise to *a second level of perception—feeling.*

The infant human being registers its sense experiences and stores them as memory. Pleasure produces the feeling *good.* Displeasure, caused by pain or fear (constriction), produces the feeling *bad.*

The experiences that the infant has with itself or its environment create *the level of feeling as premonition of that which it would like to strive for or avoid.* Its experiences and reactions, combined with what it senses and feels, already form an "opinion," or what I shall call its "inner attunement," about the nature of good and bad. This inner attunement created by the linking of our faculties of sensing and feeling is the foundation of the discriminating "I."

Even the fetus can be damaged in its integrity by

overloads that affect its sense of well-being. It is still entirely dependent on its senses, and these determine its reactions. It cannot reflect on or "understand" what happens to it. It cannot interpret pain and fear. They simply confuse it. If, for instance, the mother has to disguise the fact of her pregnancy by tightly binding her clothes, she will already be traumatizing the fetus. The infant human being will feel constricted, confined, and crushed without being able to understand what is happening. Whatever it does, it will only experience limited relief as its movements will remain constricted. If the infant could talk, it might say something like this: "*I'm* incapable of making myself feel more comfortable. *I* am too weak. *I* can't manage it. *I* am doing it all wrong. *I* must keep still; otherwise it will hurt me even more."

An unborn child that has had to endure such a constriction of its living space and mobility for an extended period of time will, as a result of the pain and fear it experiences, become intimidated, oppressed, and insecure, its personality damaged. If the human being can find no adequate outlet in response to recurrent incidents causing pain and fear, or if he cannot find ways to adapt to the situation, a latent reaction will be created in the organism. This results, consciously or unconsciously, in a tendency to tension and rigid forms of behavior like playing dead or going on the attack. Thus, a latent, future-oriented reaction, functioning like a trigger mechanism, is produced. This latent reaction is bound to the primal situation. It is a defense mechanism erected in response to specific incidents and the sum of those incidents. As a result, latent fixations—for instance, for dampness or the dark, constriction or tactile sensitivity—are created and can cause fear, palpitations, organic pain, or futile exertion.

If we have been traumatized in this way, we will, in later life, fall into patterns of reaction set off by certain key features and signals. These will prevent us from freely determining our behavior. Responses and behavioral patterns that seemed to be effective in the primal situation, and that our system now regards as essential, will be maintained in adult life. Although these particular reactions did not lead to an easing of the original situation, the "system" has registered them as apparently effective.

Or to put it another way: we will be forced to act in the established way out of fear that to alter these patterns of behavior would lead to still worse. *Fear feeds on fear.* Unaware of what was enacted in the primal situation, we remain in the dark as to what happens to us in the present. One and the same fear will drive us to struggle to find a way out of the dilemma we are caught in and, at the same time, to take refuge in stasis.

The traumatization I have mapped out will lead to a narrowing of the entire personality. It will cause a constriction, created by unconscious compulsion, that will affect our behavioral patterns and the way we relate to others. Though we will not be conscious of it, the stress arising from such a situation will constantly make us feel it, like an unhealed wound. The result is a continual, though barely perceptible, feeling of unease that will drive us to a never-ending series of directionless changes. We will react to both physical and mental challenges with feelings of immobility and anxious reticence. The moment we feel threatened either from within or from without our unconscious memories will alert our survival mechanisms. The result is tension, and our system will react in the prescribed way because it only knows and has faith in this way of dealing with the situation.

This latent response is blind, part of a system of self-preservation implanted in us unconsciously and existing in a permanent state of readiness. This is why such reactions are so stubborn.

This permanent feeling of unease produces in us a blind, undirected urge to defend ourselves. Against what, we do not know, however. The resultant feelings of rage and resignation will then be labeled as helplessness and being "wicked." This in turn overloads us emotionally. As a result we then suffer from *unconscious guilt feelings.*

This underlying, uncomprehended feeling of unease drives us onto the defensive. But because the "enemy" can be neither recognized nor apprehended, all that remains to us is a constant state of defensive alert. This is blind, generalizing, and unconscious. Chance occurrences, acting as alarm signals, will trigger it at any time. Because the injury to our primal integrity occurred in a state of helplessness and was only partially, if at all, experienced at a conscious level, we will live in a constant state of fear that it will be repeated.

This blind, latent reaction has further consequences for our emotional life. Thus, for instance, our inability to find a solution to a dilemma will be registered in the system as our own weakness. We will be burdened with guilt and feelings of worthlessness, depression, and a sense of "badness." Even the unborn child can feel handicapped and constricted for no apparent reason. Pain and anxiety, fear of its surroundings, unease, and latent anger can be its birthright. To label this organism as "neurotic" or "ill" helps us very little. Both terms are, for a start, unpleasant and only serve to rigidify anxieties and fears. What matters is that, because of the injuries inflicted on us, we will have lifelong problems of adjustment. Our quality of life will be impaired. The first and second levels of our relational system—our capacity to feel and sense—will already be strained and burdened with anxiety.

Condemned to constant defensiveness, not merely sensitized but irritated, we will stumble over activities that an untroubled, self-assured person would perform with ease. It is an illusion to think that anything positive can come from the diffidence and emotional reserve caused by such injuries. An unimpaired person is free to exercise restraint when it is called for. But permanently stifled energies, generated by fear and punctuated by outbreaks of rage, cause stress and pointlessly consume our energies. A long, difficult birth will only serve to reinforce and complicate such a prenatal condition.

A child who has been thus damaged in its primal integrity may well become the object of persecution and ridicule during childhood. These fresh traumatizations serve to deepen the injury to the child's functional integrity still further. The child, of course, cannot accept this persecution and ridicule. It may be aware of being different but cannot comprehend why this should be. It cannot understand why it is being persecuted for being what it is, why it cannot change, and why no one understands it. Until it finds help, the child experiences the destructive, psychologically threatening environment with added intensity while at the same time being its helpless victim. Repeated traumatic injuries confirm these experiences at the levels of feeling and sensing, and this only serves to heighten the strain. The latent reactions stored in the child's *emotional potential* determine its behavior. We could describe it thus: "No one loves *me.* There is something wrong with *me.* Everyone else is better and more capable than *I* am. *I* am hateful and should try harder to be a better person although I don't know what more I can do. *I* must try harder. *I* must hold back and not overreach myself so that even worse doesn't happen to me. But when? How? It's high time *I* changed. It's *my own fault* that I can't resolve my problems . . ."

Out of self-preservation, these latent reactions become rigid and ready to spring into action at any time. At the same time, the world around us balks at our problems and behavior. "We are all responsible for our own actions," people will say. Or they will offer handy diagnoses. Both, of course, do nothing but aggravate the situation. The result is predictably an even greater sense of insecurity and loss of integrity.

We are now confronted with a person whose integrity has been injured:

1. at the physical level (sensing)
2. at the emotional level (feeling)
3. at the cognitive level (thinking)

These injuries are holistic. They affect the entire organism, negatively influencing our eating habits and our protective responses or flight mechanisms. The unconscious, latent, and compulsive reactions implanted in us, though severed from a conscious awareness of the original context, are maintained in a constant state of readiness to ward off perceived dangers. This drains our energies and affects our ability to concentrate and our capacity to learn. In addition, the excess burden placed on the three dimensions of the psyche will lead to the impairment of all other mental and physical functions.

Being "psychically ill" means that our original wholeness and functionality has been injured. In response to this condition, we go on the defensive, reacting unconsciously to dangers real or perceived—and usually they are the latter—with rigid patterns of behavior. Our unconscious compulsions cause us to suffer and place unreasonable demands on others. Unable to help ourselves and weighed down with feelings of guilt, we unwittingly become a burden on the world around us.

Memories

A human being—in other words our biological system—is composed of memories—memories born of experiences compiled in the organism by numerous biological systems. These may even reach back beyond the origins of mankind. These biological memories form the basis of our physical being. They are also referred to as our hereditary information. Memories originating in the relationship between man, as a social being, and his environment have also affected the evolution of our physical system. We call these memories arising from man's collective experience *phylogenetic memories.* Our individual memories are our *ontogenetic memories.*

Our physical and emotional experiences are what form our individual memories. In each new life, collective and individual experiences become memories. This process involves the constant restructuring of body and soul. Everything that happens to us will be recorded as memories, though not always consciously. Even then, experiences transformed into memories make up an integral part of our inner "knowledge." Many memories, particularly those arising in childhood, are stored not as conscious experiences but as simply having happened. The appropriate brain functions capable of processing conscious experience were not yet fully developed as the appropriate words and concepts did not exist.

All painful and *Angst*-inducing experiences, albeit in fragmentary form, are also stored as memories and can be made conscious during the therapeutic process. It is possible to restore memories to consciousness reaching right back to the womb.

"Now I know what happened to me."

Sickness Spreads

As a child, I played at the water's edge and had the experience that stone was hard and cold to the touch. When I hit my finger with a stone, I felt an "unpleasant sensation." At first my mother called this a "boo-boo." Later she referred to it as "pain." In all, the stone gave me three experiences that conveyed to me the nature of stone and my own reactions. The sense of hardness and cold, combined with the experience of pain, formed my inner conception of the object "stone." Via my optical impressions of the form and color of the stone, this experience with stone remained in my memory as the sum of my perceptions. This memory will be revived by any object similar to the one in this first experience—in other words a comparable stone—though I may not be conscious of the process. My way of dealing with the experience will be automatic. My system already "knows" what sort of experience "stone" was for me. This initial stone experience will then transfer my expectations from stone to stone like a series of internal stepping stones.

In everyday life, such transferences take place continually. When we encounter particular objects, for instance "people with signs," which elicit certain conceptions and experiences, a particular kind of event will be anticipated. Naturally, the transference from person to person is more complicated than that from stone to stone. But despite, and perhaps because of, man's instinctive, phylogenetic expectations, transferences from person to person are more difficult to "read."

On the one hand, we inherit phylogenetic expectations. We do not expect, for instance, to be eaten by other members of the human race. On the other hand, we transfer from one person to the next our individual experiential values and "signs": that is, signs and behavioral patterns that we encounter in the present. These experiential values, combined with a person's "signs" (the object, in this context) and the resultant signals, affect our behavior consciously or unconsciously. In particular, they affect our likes and dislikes. The multiplicity of these signs can often evoke contradictory signals.

Consider the following illustration: we may feel enchanted by a sweet-smelling rose. But if we feel its thorns, our pleasure rapidly wanes and may even completely disappear (depending on how deeply the thorns have punctured the skin).

"Signs" as preconditions for something visual are initially neutral. Our inner orientational "map" only comes into existence when we endow these signs with a specific meaning shaped by our inner sensations and feelings. It is these "signs" that convey to us one or more experiences with a similar object or being, e.g., a certain person. Thus, they fulfill a crucial function. Combinations of "signs" are internalized in the form, or "Gestalt," of a symbolic value. For instance: from the sum of experiences associated with the maternal breast a symbolic evaluation of "sweet, warm, protecting roundness" is formed.

Man's highly developed sensorium and his extraordinary capacity for differentiation make a great many valuations possible, the majority of which evolve unconsciously.

Our behavior and relationships, whether in thought or in direct contact with others, are shaped by our map of internalized concepts, symbols, and images. To lead our lives we need this inner map drawn by our own individual experience. Our experiential expectations are rooted in (1) our instinctive life, that is, our phylogenetic experiences, and (2) our uniquely personal, ontogenetic experiences. We compose our internal image of a person from signs, sensations, and feelings that we have perceived in our encounters with him or her after we have "grasped" a person visually, aurally, phonetically, tactilely, and kinesthetically. Or, to put it another way: we accumulate experiences in our dealings with other people and link these to our perceptions—perceptions composed of signs such as a person's voice, hairstyle, smell, way of moving, and so on. The unconscious and conscious experiences we have recorded and stored become the vehicles and components of the totality of impressions contained in our inner map. This inner map, which is endowed with value by being linked to our sensations and feelings, forms the basis of our stance toward life. In turn, it determines our behavioral patterns and what we expect from relationships. Experiences in a specific environment with things or people that manifest particular, though variable, signs will become linked to one another. These determine the foundation of our way of orientating and our system of "transferences." We need this kind of transference in order to avoid or repeat an imminent or necessary relational act. Sensory perception is necessary to us to enable us to orient ourselves and interact. In the first instance, we transfer our perceptions and the value we have attributed to them uncritically to other relational objects that manifest similar qualities and "sign language" to those of our previous experience.

In so doing there is no guarantee that our stance, expectations, and demands are commensurate with the new encounter. This will even be the case if the person is markedly similar to others encountered in previous experiences. So it may happen that we project onto that person inappropriate attitudes (prejudices) based on characteristics we have perceived in others. If the prior experience is derived from a time of immature consciousness, it will be necessary for us to check what is happening. Impressions formed in us from early stages of our development, when our intentions, goals, and actions are not yet available to conscious recognition and we are helpless against abuse or inattentiveness, can often be misleading. We only become capable of correcting attitudes developed as a result of such transference once we have grasped the mechanisms involved and focused our efforts on carefully weighing the processes at work within us. In fleeting encounters or insignificant contacts, it is neither possible nor necessary to scrutinize our internalized system of evaluation in the transference process. This would require of us too much conscious attention—attention needed in the first instance for our protective and flight mechanisms, for the coordination of such biological drives as reproduction, mobility, the integration of experience, and our excretive functions. These priorities inhibit the fully conscious appraisal of an encounter the moment conflict arises. When one or another of these essential drives is intensified, our powers of discrimination become muddied by unconscious transferences.

Transferences influenced by the unconscious anticipation of pain or anxiety hamper our ability to form relationships and can, under certain circumstances, be critical to our survival.

In psychotic behavior, conscious appraisal of the process of transference is almost entirely absent. Uncontrollable urges gain the upper hand, and the conflict becomes loaded with a crippling expectation of pain and/or anxiety. Neurotic or psychotic forms of behavior arise from an attitude of expectation invested with an extreme degree of transference disturbance.

Chaotic transferences take place at the unconscious level, and the resultant outbreaks of rage, anger, distress, and fear usually have little or nothing to do with the real situation. When signs and signals sound a warning that a hurtful or fear-inducing experience is imminent, a state of anticipation is produced in us that causes defensiveness, withdrawal, or even aggression.

The relationship spells danger. If, by contrast, we encounter a person who signals positive experiences, we will do all we can to gain from it by repeating the experience.

Only if our expectations are conscious and sentient, and are not burdened by unconscious fears and anxieties, can our transferences be neutral and we ourselves free to "wait and see." Only after we are actively involved in sorting out the diffuse sensations and feelings prompted by the immediate experience will we be able to establish open, realistic relationships.

Because they are bound to objects, i.e., to specific persons, each with his or her characteristics, positive or negative experiences will influence, by conscious or unconscious transference, our relations to every other person. Because their effects are lasting, such experiences can enhance, inhibit, threaten, or even prevent our relationships to others. In extreme cases, the process of transference can endanger both ourselves and others. This is the case when transferences are made unconsciously. If, however, we are in touch with ourselves at a conscious level, we will have no difficulty sorting out our feelings and sensations.

Transference can only serve a positive, self-affirming function if it is carried out at a conscious level. Otherwise, destructive and/or positive experiences are blindly transferred.

Transference take place as a result of the characteristics and experiential values we have registered in our contacts with others by recording the sensory stimuli and "signals" they give out. In our interaction with others, in our encounters and relationships, we see, smell, hear, and feel the signs and specific characteristics of the person we are relating to and his or her environment. At the same time, we feel our own state of inner attunement. Mood, perception, feeling, and sensation will be simultaneously internalized, linked, and then stored as a single experience.

The resultant memory will be activated with the appearance of an object or some part of an object belonging to this memory. This can take place in both a real or a fantasized encounter. Finally, our expectations and demands of the situation are transferred to the person or object of the new encounter. This process takes place either consciously or unconsciously.

In the early stages of our development, both self-affirming and destructive events are frequently stored unconsciously. In this way, we can, without even knowing it, become victims of our own past, burdened by the traumatic experiences it once held for us.

Primal Health—Injury—Suffering

The unconscious anticipation of fear-inducing, painful events—which we have unknowingly experienced—causes in us that which we call suffering (neurosis/psychosis/psychosomatic disorders/criminality). Suffering is the fear-laden, painful anticipation of the past. It exposes our latent, unconscious vigilance.

Defensive reactions to ward off fear are generalized mechanisms acquired in the past. They include repression, denial, reversal, justification, glossing over the truth, and projection, to name but a few. In short, they are distortions of the truth adopted because the truth as we experienced it is unbearable. Unconsciously, therefore, we don't expect the present and future to be any different from the past. These experiences have established patterns for our reactions that the organism stubbornly attempts to preserve. Psychic overloads and denial have generated unconscious tendencies in us that can in some cases lead to total denial or destruction. Isn't it high time that we finally realized how far-reaching are the consequences of injury to our primal integrity? It is frightening to see how our ability to live and establish relationships with others can be damaged by disregard for our primal vulnerability.

Both physical and psychic injury, inflicted on us unconsciously, combined with apparently groundless suffering, determine how much energy we have and how we put it to use. Whether we shape our lives constructively or destructively depends on our own individual reactions, both conscious and latent-unconscious. These in turn are linked to our primal experiences. Thus, we may not, for instance, be consciously aware of a tendency to want to destroy others because this destructive tendency may be rooted in a long-forgotten experience that causes us what I will call "dis-ease"—a state that, though unnoticed and barely felt, is nonetheless potent.

Primal Vulnerability

Disregard and abuse of our primal vulnerability causes suffering and the disturbance of our ability to form relationships.

The illustration (see page 30) showing the circuit of development of human needs, commencing with the needs themselves and progressing toward fulfillment, is a visual representation of the way a person can suffer fundamental injury to his system.

The child's dependency, which arises from its cognitive weakness (visible in the third position, "object appraisal," in the first figure) includes, among other things, the child's as-yet-undeveloped ability to think, its inability to express concepts in words, and its incapacity to recognize and comprehend the motives underlying the actions of adults. As a consequence of its dependency, the child is forced to repress and "forget" the abuse it suffers, for it is unable—i.e., too weak—to adequately protect itself. It is thus almost completely at the mercy of the adults surrounding it.

Circuits and Circuit-Breakers

The first figure on page 30 shows the circuit of healthy development, beginning with the need and progressing toward the recuperative resting phase.

In the second figure, one can trace how an injury arises, thereby breaking the circuit and impairing vital needs. The ability to rest and recuperate has at this point been disturbed, and /or there exists a residual tension that continuously disrupts our inner harmony. This stage already represents the condition of someone who is suffering.

The third figure shows the disrupted circuit. It shows how the flow pattern has changed as a result of an injury. Disturbances to and the masking of the natural fulfillment of needs via perversions will be described in a subsequent chapter. Individual perversions are nothing other than reactions to injury. They originate as attempts to escape or avoid disturbances of our primal integrity. Fear, pain, and feelings of failure are contributory causes.

Study the figures, your own primally intact, integrated circuit, and think back on your past. Try to locate disturbances and encroachments on your primal integrity that may have led to injuries and overloads.

Dealing with Suffering

The Circuit: Health—Hurt—Suffering

Case 1. Normal/Healthy

In the beginning, there is . . .

the need → **searching behavior** → **object appraisal** → **pleasure, satisfaction** → **relaxation** → **rest** → **the need**

Case 2. Injury

In the beginning, there is . . .

the need → **searching behavior** → **object "blindness" as a primary or secondary weakness** → **injury/pain without the possibility of recognizing its cause** → **fear (guilt, anxiety)** → **susceptibility to cramps** → **the need**

Case 3. Suffering (reaction to injury)

In the beginning, there is . . .
the need or (now)

perversion → **search for avoidance or change** → **susceptibility to cramps in anticipation of pain caused by the unknown** → **. . . painpleasurepain . . . acting out, attempts to achieve satisfaction deviating from normal behavior, substitute needs** → **mounting tension (punishment-pain)** → **hatred (fear and anger) (Final Stage*)** → **perversion**

*Final stage also includes despair, resignation, sorrow, exhaustion, rage, and the like.

The Healthy-Hurt-Suffering chart can be used for all types of needs:

1. for cognitive needs: understanding—true information that matches reality
2. for emotional needs: our feelings—you're okay, successful, that's the way, etc.
3. for somatic needs: our physical level—corresponding to our sensations

Unconscious fear is always the fruit of injury.

Fear is transformed into personalized patterns of defensive behavior designed to guarantee survival.

The unavoidable consequence of injury to our primal integrity is suffering.

By becoming conscious of our initial vulnerability and the reactions that should have taken place in the primal scene, the suffering can be alleviated or even resolved.

The Resolution of Specific Manifestations of Suffering

One might, for instance, resolve . . . a compulsion to serve, when the person is no longer unconsciously compelled to serve; or a compulsion to keep silent; an antithinking compulsion; an antifeeling compulsion; an antisensing compulsion. All these can be resolved so that we are free to speak or think, feel or sense, when and how we want. As a result, we will be able to enter into and shape experiences involving our feelings and senses freely and without fear and in a way that is beneficial for us.

Resolving suffering means no longer being unconsciously compelled to follow, "love," or serve; not having to despair, hate, rage, or suffer. It means an end to tantrums and mournful feelings, resignation, and obedience. It means no longer being driven by fear or exhaustion. It means being able to freely, consciously, and resolutely shape our own lives and allow ourselves to love what is genuinely worthy of love.

In the first figure (normal/healthy), it is readily apparent how the satisfaction of our needs evolves from initial exploratory behavior to object appraisal. The object determines whether or not the satisfaction of a need will be pleasurable and hence lead to the desired relaxation. Following a successful interaction, we can rest until a new need arises.

For example: An infant is hungry and searches for its mother, who reacts *adequately* to its needs. This constitutes the first step in object appraisal. It seeks and finds its mother's breast and pleasurably drinks the milk until, satiated and relaxed, it smiles up at her. It allows her to rock it to sleep. After a period of rest, it will awaken and smile, searching once more for its mother in pleasant anticipation.

In the second figure—the damaged circuit—we can see how, in the third phase (object appraisal), the child is at the mercy of adults and may, as a result of its vulnerability, suffer injury. I call the child's helplessness, its lack of experience and dependency, "object blindness." Because of the child's vulnerability vis-à-vis the adult world, it can be arbitrarily hurt. The attempted satisfaction of the child's needs—which should be a pleasurable event—becomes, as a result of the injury, a painful experience the causes of which the child has no means of discovering. The child is "all need" and must obey this imperative. Every rejection, every denial, constitutes an abuse. Regardless of the reasons for the abuse, the child feels the injury as the result of its own inadequacy.

An example of such an injury: An infant is hungry. It calls out, screams, but the mother reacts only with impatience. She hastily heats the baby's bottle, barely bothering to check the temperature of the milk, then, frowning, grabs up the child. The infant, its face streaming with tears, reluctantly opens its mouth and tries to reject the hot liquid with little or no success. If the milk is too hot, it will overstimulate or even burn the mucous membranes in the infant's mouth. Not only will the pain/heat threshold be arbitrarily raised; "toughening up" the child like this will also lead to the creation of a habit that is at variance with physiological realities. The abnormally raised tolerance for heat can lead directly or gradually to organic damage. (In addition, it serves to pave the way for smoking and other overstimulating perversions.) Instead of meeting with the expected, pleasurable satisfaction of its need, the child is subjected to pain—pain inflicted by its mother or someone else entrusted with its care, in other words the very person from whom the child expects precisely the opposite, namely help and comfort. The child will store the memory of a grim face staring accusingly at it. In the future, as soon as the child senses a need, it will be gripped by fear and vainly attempt to escape the situation. The injuries inflicted upon its body and soul (in this case, massive damage to the first and second levels) give rise to latent overreactions in the system that constitute a burden and simultaneously generate constant fear.

(Self-)Damnation

Pain and disappointment cause feelings of anxiety and guilt in the child. *My system has failed,* the child's internal monitors warn from now on. As a result, the child will develop a fear of its own needs. Because experience has taught its system to expect injury, the child becomes tense as soon as it senses a need. It will develop a fear of those who care for it while simultaneously idealizing them for as long as possible as a means of self-preservation. The repetition of experiences like this will gradually transform the child. Its self-esteem, the foundation of all human activity, will be turned into self-doubt. A healthy life will be made unlivable. The child, made permanently insecure, will from now on hardly be able to relax. It will be plagued by unconscious guilt feelings, and it will suffer.

The third figure: suffering. Here the following process can be observed—as soon as vital needs can no longer be suppressed in the child's system, it is impelled to somehow find satisfaction for them. This urge, though, at the same time triggers anxiety-induced tensions or even cramps. The child's experience has taught it to anticipate pain when it senses and feels a need, and it naturally desires to avoid that pain. As soon as the need becomes stronger than the anticipation of fear and pain, the child will be willing to accept substitute gratification. In so doing, it gives itself up to the dictates and terms of its environment. If things come to a head, the child, already accustomed to pain and self-sacrifice, may even die. The anger, rage, and despair born of the unsuccessful and painful satisfaction of its needs will, along with feelings of guilt, hatred, and anxiety, be unconsciously registered by the child's system as *its own* inability to adjust. The entire sequence of events, linked with whatever perceptions it has gained from its surroundings, will be stored. The outcome is a tense, suffering child, prone to cramps and programmed for defensiveness, a child who goes in fear of the unconscious hatred and rage stored in it as a result of its experience, but who is unable to help itself. Such a child dreads the dawn of every new day.

An example of suffering: The infant awakes screaming from a bad dream, its face scarlet. The mother responds, but only automatically, with little affection. In truth, she detests the child. She performs her duty perfunctorily, not out of love for the child but out of fear of chastisement. The infant seeks nourishment but simultaneously wishes it could refuse. It has already awakened in fear and pain. Now it expects more of the same. The search for relief combined with the drive to self-defense create a tortuous, vicious circle. As a result, the infant receives its nourishment in a state of pain and compulsion. Its body tenses up even more and its desperation increases because, however it tries to adapt to the situation, it cannot achieve real satisfaction. The child therefore becomes exhausted, sad, and confused, and the person caring for it will leave it feeling disgruntled. Worn out and afraid of everything (both within itself and around it), the child falls asleep.

What Lurks Behind Fear

As long as we suffer from tensions caused by injuries, psychic overloads, or deprivation, our lives are at the mercy of the past. Blindly following its dictates, our behavior governed by unconscious transferences, we live in constant danger.

In the figure showing the phase of suffering (see page 30), we are trapped in the *final position.* Our energies are consumed by warding off old dangers. Unfortunately, we are barely aware of everything that is happening in us. What is more, the intensity of our feelings usually escapes us. Our ever-ready, latent reactions function like a secretly programmed time bomb set to detonate in response to certain signals. But as the bomb's programmers neglected to inform us what they were, these signals remain unknown to us. Every time the bomb threatens to explode, feelings are released in us that set off an alarm, mobilize our defenses, and set us on edge. The reasons for this whole procedure, though, remain obscured from us. Naturally, the almost unbearable physical and emotional strains inherent in the situation, coupled with our feelings of hatred and self-hatred, cause us to suffer. To regain our health, it is necessary for us to open up to all our feelings and sensations. We must repress nothing and focus instead on how, why, where, and by whom they were caused. All our feelings, both positive and negative—but, above all, violent hate feelings and compulsive desires—are dependable trail markers on the path to our past. We must follow this trail back to its source to enable us to identify the origins of our problems and resolve our blind urges and our distress. Rage, anxiety, despair, sorrow, exhaustion, hate, resignation—these are all sure signs of psychic distress. Our fear is the sum of these writs served on us by our past.

The latent, destructive power we harbor within us is strong and dangerous in proportion to the severity of the primal injuries inflicted on us. Old destructive powers work on in us like a ticking bomb. They were created in the victim: the abused child.

The Therapy

The term *primal therapy* gives an idea of what takes place during therapy, namely a supportive reevaluation of our primal relationships and the problems that arise from them. Its aim is to resolve primally induced anxiety, pain, and confusion by uncovering their origins. That involves a lonely confrontation with our parents and other "primal persons."

Primal therapy is a self-help therapy that can be learned. It requires discipline and the ability to see something through. The therapy examines past events in order to actively and consciously experience them in the present.

At our center, the process consists of a "basic" therapy followed by group therapy. On average, the basic sequence consists of twenty to twenty-five full days within a period of four to five weeks. Daily sessions last up to three hours. The rest of the day is devoted to rest and individual work, such as reviewing therapy tapes. The subsequent group therapy takes place under the supervision of a therapist in five-hour sessions conducted once a week. This part of the therapy usually lasts from several months to several years.

After an initial period, some people are able to continue the therapy independently. Group therapy is only in order when essential insights have been gained in the basic period. The group situation is stimulating and makes other people's experience available to us.

Primal therapy means self-growth. At the same time, it is a learning method aimed at enabling us to reappraise and resolve our confusions and difficulties in personal relationships. What has been only passively endured becomes consciously experienced. Our memories become conscious.

The result is an awareness that gives us access to our thoughts, feelings, and sensations. In the course of therapy, we become conscious of our latent potential. With time, we are able to go into relationships with a relaxed, realistic outlook that enables us to react in a healthy, constructive way.

The length of the healing process varies greatly from person to person and is not determined exclusively by the therapy itself. Persons who are severely afflicted may have to do work on themselves for many years before they become capable of leading a coherent, fulfilling existence.

The Therapist

Therapists working with this form of therapy must have a good, general education. Because of the training they receive, doctors and psychologists are normally best qualified to work as therapists. They must have reached a level in their own personal therapy where they are able to respond adequately to any problem that may arise. They must have a grounding in evolution, psychology, and physiology. They should be free of fear, capable of facing the anxiety and pains of their own childhoods and of knowing how to deal with them. They must be genuine, centered people themselves. People with addictions or inordinate vanities cannot become good primal therapists. Nor can those living in dependent relationships in which they deny their own needs or allow themselves to be abused. Therapists are dangerous if they deny that they too are only human and presume to know better what happened in a patient's life. They need to have a degree in "the university of life" and be able to intuitively grasp the problems of those who come to them for help. Therapists who have no patience with those in their care have no business being therapists. Good therapists are also willing to apologize for mistakes and do not leave misunderstandings unclarified. They must be sensitive, knowledgeable people. They must be helpful and understanding. To be a therapist is a difficult, demanding job, and only those who are themselves stable can be expected to have to face the most hideous, unbelievable, and bizarre aberrations of human nature. I believe that only if we regard it as a contribution to the evolution of mankind can we do justice to this work.

Prerequisites for Therapy

A prerequisite for therapy is to determine whether a course of psychotherapy is appropriate or whether a person's suffering is caused by organic illness. A thorough medical examination is an absolute must. Ultimately, the person seeking help will decide for him- or herself whether to enter therapy.

Primal therapy is by definition taxing, involving as it does a thorough confrontation with the past. A readiness to go through with that process "come what may" is an essential requirement of any therapy because there is a high probability that in the course of it one will be confronted with terrible, dreadful realities. Despite that, it is a constructive process.

Finding the right person to work with can be compared to finding the right midwife. In both cases, the job can only be done by someone who wants "the child." If such a person cannot be found, it is essential that we create a therapist *within ourselves*. That this is possible has been proved by those who have had the courage to make the attempt—and been successful. The therapy can be learned with the guidelines presented in this book.

The tragedy of the unloved child is so terrible because the child has no way at all of grasping what has happened to it. Child neglect runs counter to all the dictates of Nature. For such a child it is almost *unbearable* to have to face how it was constantly unloved;

how, instead, it was abused, exploited, and threatened; beaten, frightened, and rejected when it wanted one thing only: to be loved. At the end of all this, a child is likely to regard any affection as a ruse and, sensing danger, resist it. The unloved child cannot fathom that, instead of being loved by those on whom its life depended, it was hated. Its system will be programmed to, above all, avoid danger. In so doing, it avoids life itself. The joy of being alive is drowned in a bitter sea of silence. Is all that remains a zombielike existence in the ranks of the living dead? The answer is no. With the help of therapy, we can free ourselves from the dead hand of the past. But we have to take that step ourselves.

The Initial Interview

It is important to establish whether the patient wishes to work with the given therapist and whether the therapist is willing and able to help the patient in question. In addition, the financial side of things must be settled. When you have found a therapist willing to work with you, there will probably be a period of waiting. You will send in a full outline of your life history and be asked to fill in a series of questionnaires asking for information your therapist will require.

The Therapeutic Procedure

The work is carried out in trusting cooperation with the therapist. Patients should have a suitable living situation that allows them to go into "retreat" and commune with themselves. Ideally, a patient would live in the therapy center itself, but this entails maintenance costs and investment.

During the basic therapy, certain rules need to be observed. These will be drawn up by the therapist and contain guidelines as to abstinence, working conditions, and other recommendations linked to the therapy.

Therapy begins with a review of one's life story, which should be written down in as much detail as possible. Start with a description of your parents' lives before marriage. A simple genealogical tree traced back to your grandparents' generation will give you an initial overview. Briefly compile your own personal data in a table and illustrate them with situational sketches. Plans of your childhood home and its environment are a helpful aid to memory (see the samples provided on pages 51–53).

Instructions for the Basic Therapy

The patient is given these instructions prior to the beginning of the therapy. They should be followed at all times. If you fail to observe these rules, though, you have not committed a crime. They are intended to help you and to promote the success of the therapy so that the therapist is in an optimal position to help you. However, it is important to inform him or her of any departure from these guidelines:

1. Smoking and alcohol are to be discontinued twenty-four hours before the start of therapy. These habits are debilitating. You are going to need all your energy to become well again.
2. Sleeping pills and any other medication should be discontinued upon commencing therapy.
3. The twenty-four hours prior to the commencement of therapy should be spent alone. You can use the time to go through the therapy documentation or go for walks, but do not seek any other forms of distraction.

   Sexual activity is to be discontinued—not because we view it as unhealthy per se, but because abstinence enhances therapy. For this reason, you are asked to report any departures from this rule.

   Everything you are asked to do is designed to help you get in touch with your feelings and sensations as far as possible. Make notes in your diary or journal so that, if you consider it helpful, you can give them to the therapist to read. Record what happens and how you feel. Note down your recollections of the past.
4. When you are in therapy, try to voice everything you are feeling and thinking without blocking anything out. You can ask anything you wish to know and will always be given an honest answer. Please tell the therapist when

you are tired. No therapy can be productive if a patient is tired.

5. You will be allotted three hours of therapy per day. However, either you or the therapist can interrupt the session at any time should it be necessary.

   The remainder of the day will be spent resting and working over the results of the therapy session. You can listen to the recordings made in the therapy session. But do stop as soon as you tire. Later, when you are refreshed, you can pick up again where you left off. Continuity is important when listening to the tapes. Make notes about the therapy and continue to supplement your autobiographical sketch. As soon as you are able, draw up the sketches and tables recommended in the documentation: that is, your genealogical tree, a table of significant events, and floor plans of your home situation. Supplement your personal profile with an account of your parents' lives before their marriage.
6. Rest as much as possible. Take walks. If you wish to do sports, please discuss this in advance with your therapist. Check and recheck to make sure that you have provided all information necessary for the therapy.

   Read and re-read the therapy documentation. Everything you say will be kept in the strictest confidence. Psychotherapists are bound by law to confidentiality. Access to information you disclose about yourself will be prohibited to third parties.
7. Call your therapist whenever you need him or

her. You should keep the telephone numbers by your phone.

8. In your own interest, all these instructions should be conscientiously followed. Please do not hesitate to ask if there is anything you do not understand.

The Setting

The room in which therapy takes place should be specially soundproofed and upholstered so that physical outbursts are no cause for concern. The temperature of the room should be moderate and the room itself painted in dark colors. It should be equipped with adjustable lighting and a tape recorder with adjustable recording levels. (See also page 113.)

Whenever possible, therapy should be conducted in an absolutely dark, quiet room. This enhances perception and allows memories to "come to light" more clearly. The patient should be able to stretch out comfortably without feeling restricted in his or her movements in any way.

"Life Maps"

The unconscious anticipation of fear-inducing, painful events we have unknowingly experienced in the past causes what we refer to as "suffering."

Suffering is the anxious/painful anticipation of the past and consists of our latent, unconscious reactions.

Family Genealogy

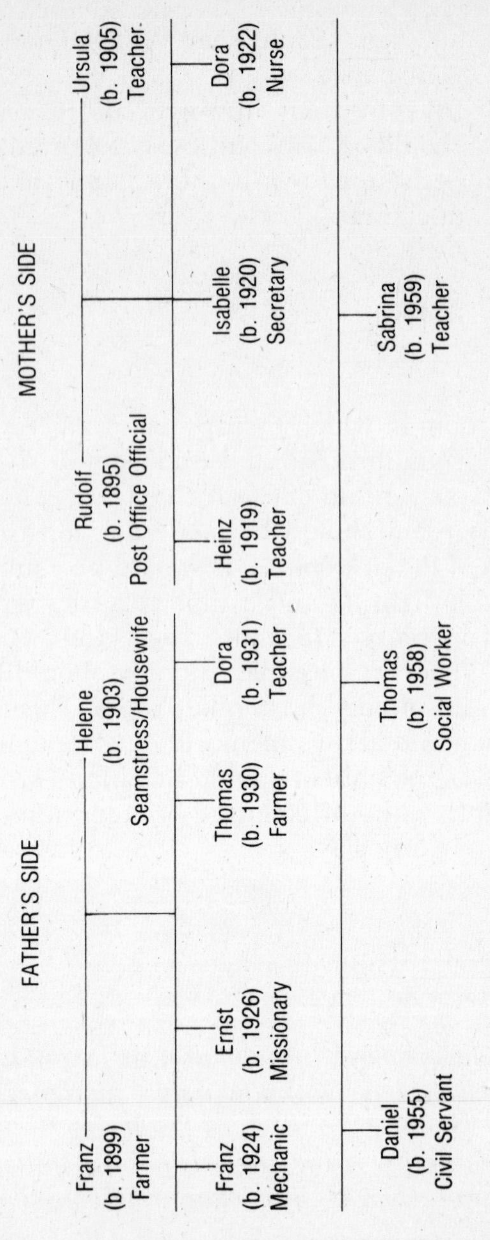

Family Life Chart

YEAR 19—	54	55	56	57	58	59	60	61	62	63	64	65	66	67	68	69	70	71
FATHER Franz 1/3/24	Quiet, hard-working, hot-tempered, transparent																	
AGE FOUNDLING	30	31	32	33	34	35	36	37	38	39	40	41	42	43	44	45	46	47
MOTHER Dora 8/6/22	Plays the saint but manipulates her husband and children																	
AGE	32	33	34	35	36	37	38	39	40	41	42	43	44	45	46	47	48	49
BROTHER Daniel 10/10/55	Mother's favorite; his colleagues are more important to him																	
AGE		0	1	2	3	4	5	6	7	8	9	10	11	12	13	14	15	16
Thomas 2/9/58	Breech Birth '58; 14 days in the clinic																	
AGE					0	1	2	3	4	5	6	7	8	9	10	11	12	13
SISTER Sabrina 3/17/59	Father's favorite; demands a lot of herself																	
AGE						0	1	2	3	4	5	6	7	8	9	10	11	12

YEAR 19—	72	73	74	75	76	77	78	79	80	81	82	83	84	85	86	87	88	89
FATHER Franz 1/3/24																		
AGE FOUNDLING	48	49	50	51	52	53												
MOTHER Dora 8/6/22						Guilt feelings, arthritis												
AGE	50	51	52	53	54	55	56	57	58	59	60	61	62	63	64	65	66	67
BROTHER Daniel 10/10/55																		
AGE	17	18	19	20	21	22	23	24	25	26	27	28	29	30	31	32	33	34
Thomas 2/9/58																		
AGE	14	15	16	17	18	19	20	21	22	23	24	25	26	27	28	29	30	31
SISTER Sabrina 3/17/59																		
AGE	13	14	15	16	17	18	19	20	21	22	23	24	25	26	27	28	29	30

This table is designed as a memory aid. The years are noted on the top line, followed by the parents and children according to age. You should give yourself the most room for notes on:

- special events
- school
- illnesses
- moves
- accidents
- friends
- operations
- enemies, etc.

HOME SITUATION 1

Daniel is between 0 and 2 years old.

We try to become conscious of our home situation during childhood by drawing up floor plans of our surroundings at the time.

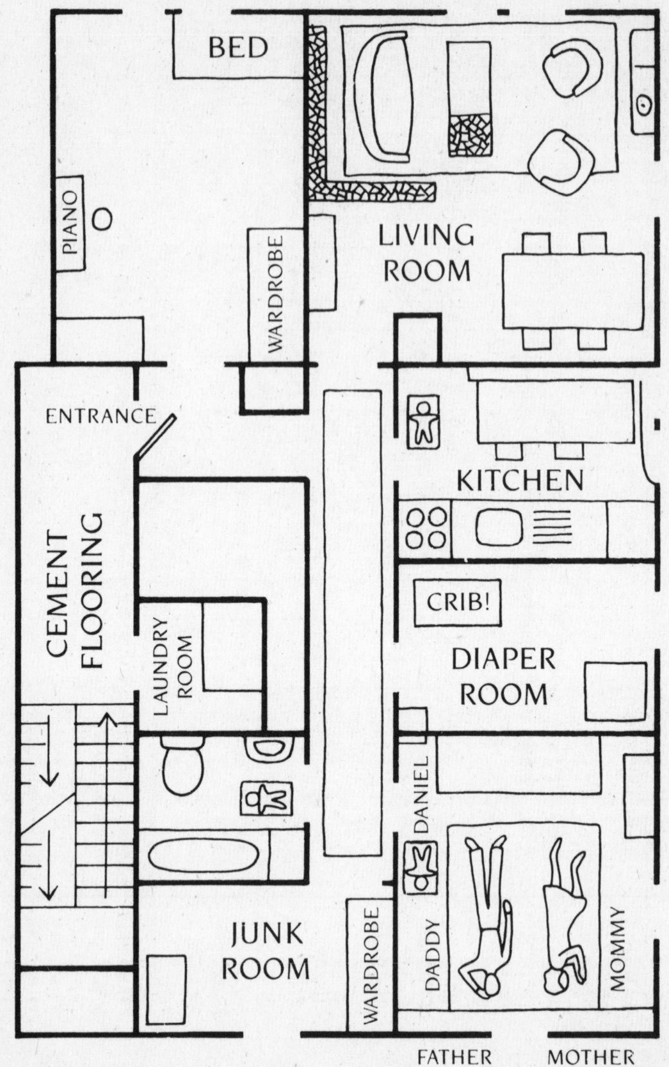

HOME SITUATION 2

Daniel is age 5, Thomas 2, and Sabine 1.

Daniel and Thomas slept in the same bed until Sabine was born.

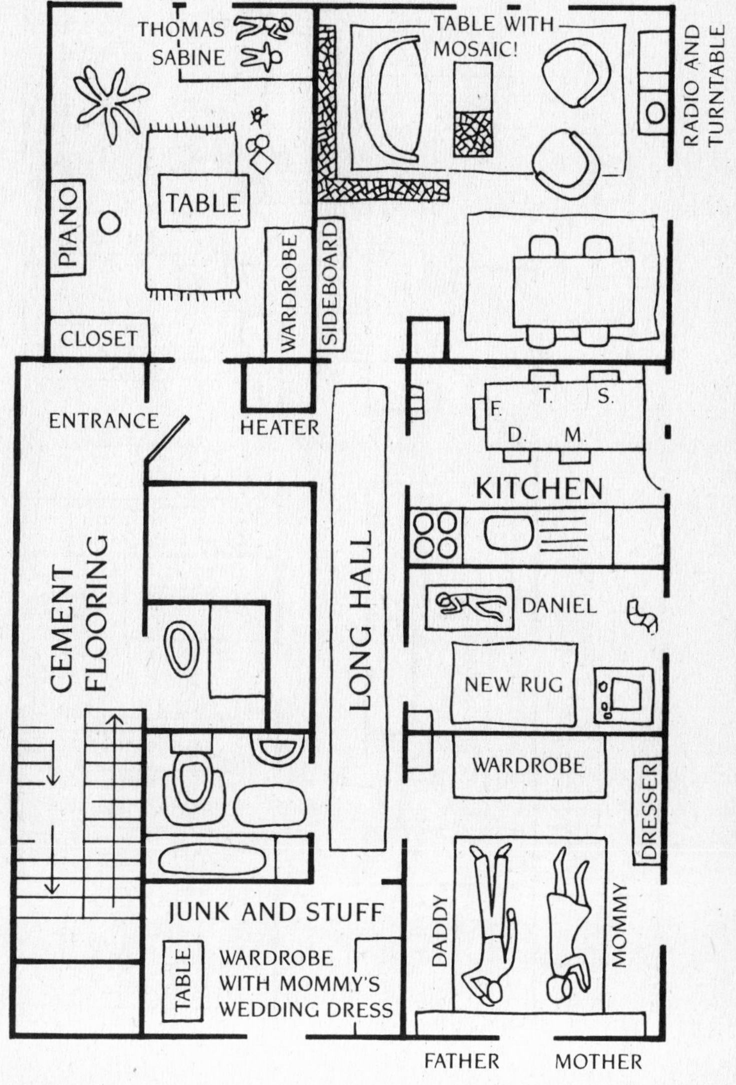

HOME SITUATION 3

Daniel is age 14, Thomas 11, and Sabine 10.

Thomas and Sabine shared the same bed until Thomas was about 5 years old.

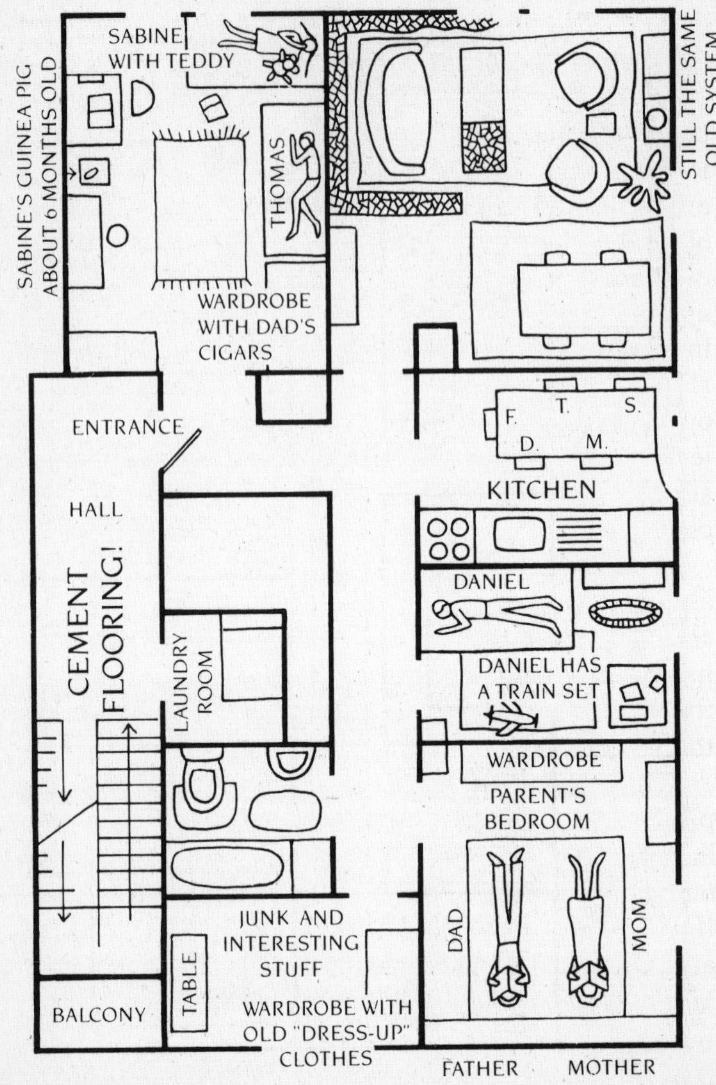

The Child's Advocate

You are now to become the advocate of the hurt child—the advocate of the child within you who, from fear of unconscious dangers, is constantly influencing you, preventing you from acting independently and determining your own destiny. The therapist knows how persistent transference is and how it constantly projects feelings, opinions, and sensations onto the world around us. In primal therapy transference also affects our relations with the therapist. This is unavoidable even when we do not deliberately apply it in the therapeutic process. It helps greatly if you voice your feelings as freely as possible even when it might seem risqué, rude, or impudent. Don't censure yourself. Be open. You will meet with neither punishment nor rejection. Therapy is there to sort out our inner confusion. To create order, though, we first have to take a closer look at the disorder within us.

The need to lash out at the therapist should be voiced as soon as possible. The moment you feel threatened or constrained by your therapist, you should say so. Feelings always have reasons. If they are not appropriate to the immediate situation, they can be effectively assigned to their real context.

The first steps are always the hardest. The therapist can begin to help and offer support as soon as he has a good grasp of your history and has comprehended your specific problematic. He will accompany the therapy step by step. So that you can review and augment your experiences in therapy the sessions will be taped. Try to do this reviewing on a regular basis but only when you feel receptive and capable of really giving your attention to the recordings.

During therapy you should keep your eyes closed. Even in a darkened room, shadows can still be a distraction. Hypersensitivity or fear may prevent you from being able to keep your eyes closed. If this is the case, it is crucial to go into this and talk about it. Keeping your eyes closed improves concentration and allows you to "see" images from your memories more clearly. Our ability to remember varies from person to person. Some people feel they can "see" whole scenes, like watching a movie. Others may never, out of fear and anxiety, have been permitted to look their parents and guardians in the eye. As a result many patients are initially occupied with recalling the past by describing it as fully as possible. Often a partial recollection can bring a whole memory "back to life." Old photographs from the past can often trigger recollections of people and situations. Sometimes, while looking at a photograph, you will consciously and critically see friends and relatives for the first time.

To make progress in therapy, it is essential to establish a dialogue with significant others from the past and the present—a dialogue in the literal sense, which you conduct aloud with people you remember. This dialogue is composed of your statements and the answers given by the people in these "talks." You yourself will supply these responses from your recollection of their opinions and habits, the ways they had of expressing themselves and their gestures, combined with numerous other details you automatically recorded and stored without, at that time, being able to consciously process this material. Using this dialogue form you will, as soon as you are able to, begin to clarify current incidents. The same method will then be applied to uncover and work through the interactions that took place in your childhood. In this way you become in a very real sense the *child's advocate.* By bringing our adult point of view to bear on the dialogue, we free the child in us from unwarranted, unconscious guilt feelings by confronting and correcting the false opinions and views projected on us by the adults we knew in childhood. With no risk to ourselves, we will be able to brave the confrontation with people who were once significant for us. At last we will be able to see conflicts through to the end and develop self-protective reactions that were previously unavailable to us. In this way, many of our "views," about ourselves and others will gradually be transformed into realistic insights.

Taking as our point of departure events, moods, and feelings in the present, therapy enables us to penetrate the past. In so doing we will raise our consciousness of the feelings and sensations associated with the original situations. Initially, there is a powerful defensive reaction against the realities of the past. This lasts until we are better placed to gain insight into these painful events. In the course of time, we become capable of giving expression to previously repressed reactions. We learn to understand ourselves and resolve our problems. Every therapeutic interaction, carried through within the four-step procedure, sheds light on past events and gradually begins to ease the tensions and problems rooted in our relational conflicts. The events and incidents we go through become experiences from which we can mold a growing sense of reorientation and autonomy.

As children, we were either unable to conduct such a dialogue or never allowed to learn how. In some cases we even had to "unlearn" this innate ability. Thus, it is crucial that we relearn and practice such dialogues. With time we will rediscover a balanced ability to freely act and react. Thereafter, we will be in command of our natural, self-enhancing capabilities and functions. Everything we do will no longer be subject to the tyranny of fear.

We will be able to react to pain and fear with increased consciousness. As we feel and give expression to energy set free in the therapeutic process, the link between all three relational levels (sensing, feeling, and thinking) will be restored. Sometimes this takes place in an emphatic way with verbal outbursts or screams. We may want to strike out at the air or at the upholstery of the therapy room. In this way blocked energies will be set free. Occasionally, we need to shout and scream to allow the psychosomatic current to flow and the circuit to get back on track. Pseudoactivities or "play-acted" scenes have absolutely no effect. *Only by giving expression to reactions grounded in real feelings and facts can we arrive at the long-term resolution of physical and psychic tensions.*

The practice of the four-step procedure, leading to self-enhancing behavior, must be carried out *viva voce*—in other words, in actual speech—for this allows us to constantly reexamine the interaction taking place within our system. In this way the feelings and perceptions we give voice to will be subject to our own system of self-control. They will thus modify our inner experience. In time this self-therapeutic method will be integrated into our own thought processes.

In this way we will forge new links between the "compass points" of the soul, or, to put it another way, between the body and the central nervous system. The two cerebral hemispheres—the left hemisphere, responsible for "rational thinking" and managing our pattern of reactions; and the right hemisphere, which specializes in intuitive, holistic apprehension—can be brought via therapy into a balanced, harmonizing relation with one another. The progressive clarification of feelings brings us all-round relief. Our organs will function with less strain. We will be able to be more objective. We can live our lives in closer touch with reality.

The Four Steps

The four steps are based on our inborn, primal ability to establish relationships to ourselves and the world around us.

The order of the four steps corresponds to the building blocks of our functions as they determine our interactive ability. From our sensory perceptions arise feelings and sensations. These are then "read" and understood by our internal system. This process takes place in correspondence with the phylogenetic and ontogenetic experiences we have stored, forming the basis for our reactions and interactions.

Perceptions awaken sensations and feelings in us, which are then given appropriate evaluations. These evaluations, together with the influence exerted by our intellect, govern our "steering mechanism." This gives rise to both our reactions and the articulation of our needs—our "need-demand."

In the following overview, the four steps are intentionally not described in full detail. They are guidelines and do not pretend to be complete. Each individual will conduct the dialogue with his or her own words. What is crucial, however, is that all four steps be performed in each interaction.

One might assume that, having completed the third step, the individual has gained much insight and the therapy has accomplished its goal. This, however, is not the case. Only the fourth step (for which the first three steps are the basis) can resolve unconscious events. What is the good of realizing that "my parents were such and such" without being able to realize what "such and such" meant with all its consequences—in other words, *how they really were as parents.* And this is what might happen if the examination of the question during the third step was either incompletely carried out, or not at all, and the parents, in the course of therapy, were never told how parents *should* be. Simple generalizations, of the "such and such" kind, can lead neither to a full recognition of the truth nor to a realization of what the child really needed. This can only be achieved by the fourth step.

The more deep-seated reason for unconsciousness, for repression, is that the impulses, needs, and drives, which are vitally important if we are to organize and determine our own lives, have been impaired, punished, and disrupted. These abuses were near-deadly encroachments on our primal integrity. As a result, we keep our needs more or less at an unconscious level. We live unconsciously. Being forced to repress reactive feelings against our tormentors, for fear of being further punished and threatened, is another cause of unconsciousness. For the child it was impossible to recognize who was responsible for its distress. It remained in the dark as to what was actually going on.

Even today, this causes pain and leads to essential facets of our own history remaining unconscious.

In my view, primal therapy means lifting the curtain of unconsciousness that was drawn after our primal integrity was damaged:

- in step four, because the need has been impaired;
- in step three, because this was a violation of Nature that disregarded the fact that a child still needs an umbilical cord to the world;
- in step two, because the injury caused rage and fury and other feelings. Unable to understand what happened at that time, we remain prisoners of the injury and its consequences;
- in step one, because the *end position* (see page 30) is dominated by confusion, distress, and unclarity. This prevents us from coping with new situations and encounters and being able to behave in a life-enhancing fashion.

"Success" has been achieved as soon as the symptoms disappear.

The main part of the therapy begins with a descriptive account of the way we feel.

The Four Steps in Summary

1. **Perception** (present or recalled)

In the first step, I try to describe my general condition: What I am sensing
noticing

seeing
hearing
smelling

What bothers me, what is on my mind . . .

2. **Feelings**

In the second step, I give voice to my sensations and feelings, how they affect me and what they mean:

What this means to me
does to me
causes to happen in me
leaves behind
means . . .

3. **Understanding**

In the third step, I critically examine the situation, the scene, and those involved (including myself). I demand an explanation (explain myself) and justification. I ask:

Why am I doing this? What for?
What good does it do?
Where does it come from?
Why?

What have I done wrong?
not understood?
forgotten to do?
made a mess of?

4. **Demands** (what I really need)

In the fourth step, I formulate my demands:

I don't need this . . .
I need that . . . to live.

A Note to the Third Step

Calling the behavior of others into question means questioning their actions toward *me* and the effect they have on me. How people I am relating to affect me, and what effect they have on me, needs to be examined and evaluated. The questions I pose must always be aimed at helping me discover the reasons behind their actions and behavior—but always as they directly relate to me. For instance: Why are you doing this to me? Have I given you a reason?

Setting the way that significant others behave toward us within the context of their own life histories—in other words, coming to see what in their past drove them to behave in an unwarranted way toward us—may serve to reassure us. Explanations of their behavior may help us to understand their problems. But they help us to discover *our own* truth little. Either we are blessed with the truth about ourselves from the start—in that our parents protect and care for our primal integrity—or we have to discover it laboriously.

The First Signs of Change

In the first step, you will be asked to express your current state of mind, to express in words "what is" right now. You will also be encouraged to give voice to your most urgent perception, the problem that is currently on your mind. To do this you will lie with your eyes closed as comfortably as possible on an upholstered couch in a darkened room and try to "get in touch with yourself." Let your system as a whole take over. Only allow as much of the feelings and experiences stored in you to come to the surface as you can cope with. Anything more, and your own physical mechanisms will numb you or cause you to faint. The therapist will be at your side, fully concentrated and ready to support you. He already knows the outlines of your life story and how to be of help. You will probably relate what is happening to you at the moment. The therapist will listen, only interjecting when constructive intervention seems appropriate.

For instance: "I didn't sleep well at all. I always wake up at three o'clock, even if I have only fallen asleep shortly before. Then I lie awake for an hour or two, though I am exhausted when I go to bed . . ."

In the second step, try to spontaneously describe the feelings and sensations arising from these perceptions. Describe their effects and what this means for you.

For instance: "My limbs hurt as though I had been put through a wringer. I was furious and terrified that 'it' was all going to start up again. I have often had this problem. Up to now no one has been able to help me. Even if I took sleeping pills, it didn't help . . ."

In the third step, try to unearth the reasons for your problems. Think critically about the situation, those involved and yourself.

For instance: "I didn't overexert myself in any way yesterday or the day before. I didn't do sports and I haven't drunk coffee." Here the therapist may point out that negative incidents from the past can trigger a state of wakefulness at certain times of the day or night. "A few years ago I was driving home across a mountain pass in a snowstorm. It was after my brother's wedding. There wasn't enough room for us all in the hotel, so some of us had to sleep elsewhere. Since I knew the roads, I decided to drive home over the pass. It was already the dead of night. Though it was June, there was still snow on the pass. On the way down I got caught in a blizzard. I could hardly see through the swirling mass of white. Because I had passengers with me, I was worried. But I didn't have the courage to pull over or admit that I was afraid. What's more, I was struggling to keep awake. I had to summon every ounce of energy to get those people, who had entrusted themselves to my care, down to the valley. Can this event have caused the 'alarm' function?" "That's unlikely to be the case, I think, as everything turned out all right that time." "Well, but now I remember something else: I was born at three o'clock in the morning. I hadn't even thought about that." "What sort of a birth was it?" "I asked my mother that recently, and she said it was a perfectly normal birth. After labor pains had begun, fairly mildly at first, I was delivered under normal conditions at three o'clock in the morning. My mother had gone to the clinic by taxi at three in the afternoon. They gave her laughing gas. Apparently I looked a bit blue at the beginning, but after a few hard slaps on the bottom I gave my first cry. My mother held me in her arms for the first time at seven o'clock, but she wasn't able to breast-feed me as I had such a severe case of hiccups. After I had been given some medication, I calmed down and eventually she was able to feed me. Unfortunately, I was only breast-fed for a week. My mother got an infection of the breast and I was put on a bottle. Apparently I adapted well to it."

Here the patient requires orientation from the therapist on the birth procedure and its consequences. The length of labor—twelve hours—signifies traumatization. This is evidenced in the lack of oxygen at birth (the bluish coloring). The immediate severing of the umbilical cord caused feelings of suffocation. The blows resulted in pain and fear. The child was not brought to its mother until four hours after the birth. As a consequence of the birth trauma and the immediate separation from the mother, the lack of physical contact and tactile reassurance that would tell a child "You're safe now. Everything will be all right," it remained in a state of shock. If the birth has been brutal, a child is in urgent need of immediate and sustained comfort from its mother so it can come to itself, and into the world. This birth was a hideous experience. The sensation the child is left with is one of sheer torture. As a result, its body memory tells it that "movement" and "wanting" both spell mortal danger.

Births such as these, which traumatize a child, are bound to leave behind an "alarm" effect whose function is to avert the repetition of such a threatening experience. But how could such a thing have happened? The patient now addresses his/her consternation at the mother:

"But that's awful. I had no idea that my birth was so bad and is still affecting my unconscious day and night. Mother, what was it actually like? How was it for you? Was there no one there to stand by you and tell you what was important? Why did you give yourself so utterly into the hands of the medical staff? Why were you so ignorant of what had to be done—for instance, when the umbilical cord had to be cut? Why didn't you know about any of this? Surely a woman should know the basic facts about pregnancy and birth. I mean, Dad was a doctor after all. Couldn't *he* have explained everything to you? And where was he, anyway, when I was born? On military service? And you're telling me he only got leave the day after the birth? How come? Surely he could have gotten leave earlier if he had tried. Or was it because the birth was repellent to him, just as I was almost always repellent to him? Was that it? Was Dad not there because *he didn't want* a child in the first place? It's unbelievable. My father is a doctor, but I nearly die at birth because he refuses to be there. I just don't believe it. That blows me away."

At this point the patient is probably aware for the first time of some of the feelings stemming from his primal situation. How much of his rage, pain, and indignation is articulated depends on the experience as a whole and on his willingness to confront these unsettling discoveries. The consequences of a traumatizing situation almost short-circuit our ability to comprehend it. As a result, part of the event must be repressed anew. The part that can be made available to consciousness needs a great deal of time to work through and review. This is one of the reasons for the need to explore insights of this type again and again. In day-to-day life, this need constantly arises as problems in relating to others signal that the effects of injury to our primal integrity are still with us. Naturally, it is not possible to react immediately in the appropriate way. Not only does this require a great deal of time and energy. Our system also cannot cope with everything at once. Rage, fear, pain, indignation, sorrow, desperation, and resignation have to be *shown and substantiated* in full measure before a lessening of tension can be achieved. Supposed guilt feelings must be dispelled, and a feeling of calm and reassurance established.

The convoluted, emotion-laden sequence of events, which we can compare to a tangled ball of wool, is for the first time in the process of being unraveled. It must be carefully unwound, strand by strand, and each strand must be named, sorted, and classified. The patient must now be allowed to react in the context of the primal situation. What comes naturally to a child whose consciousness has not been impaired must now be painstakingly learned.

To complete the therapy and continue to apply its principles we need a great deal of patience and persistence with ourselves and our pasts. For the child, to repress certain experiences was a matter of life and death. The simple fact of being an unloved child was unbearable, and only by repressing this knowledge was it able to survive. That is why it was necessary to banish the memory of maltreatment and attempts to murder the child from the child's store of recollections. In cases of severe injury, i.e., traumatization, our organs could literally not cope if the human system were not able to help by what we could call "self-anesthesia" and repression. For a moment, the traumatic experience is thus removed from the waking consciousness and we continue our lives as though nothing had happened. Nevertheless, the state of shock induced by past traumas can last for years or even decades. Until they become part of our conscious experience, they will continue to influence our lives.

In the fourth step, you will articulate, again within the context of the same situation, your needs and your *rightful* claim to that which would have prevented the initial damage and helped you to live.

For example: "Surely, you should have come to an agreement with each other before the pregnancy. You couldn't just have a child against Dad's will.

"You must have noticed back then how resistant he was. You wanted to have a baby for yourself—but at my expense. Afterward, when you were sick, Dad didn't come to your aid either. And, suffering as you were, you couldn't fulfill my needs. I needed you to be healthy and whole, full of enthusiasm and happiness. To this day I can remember the sadness in your face. I always felt deeply sorry for you. But I never knew what I had done wrong or how I could make it better. I needed your love to live. I needed you to be totally there for me."

Of course, the therapy does not end there. It will continue to unfold; and the therapist must ensure that the patient doesn't lose the thread. The patient is continuing "on track to himself." Only, he is not as certain of his bearings as the therapist. The therapist's certainty is based on his insights, his knowledge of the primal theory, the effectiveness of the therapy as he has experienced it, and on his experience in giving help. The life and sufferings of the patient are thus not simply a burden to the therapist. They form an essential part of the experiential background of the therapy itself.

With the completion of the four steps as illustrated here, the patient will have arrived at a new consciousness. But because every single cell and every organ, feeling, and thought are intimately related to one another, much work remains to be done. Far-reaching changes can only be achieved once the therapy has become a part of our day-to-day behavior.

The therapy is, above all, designed to enable us to

live a conscious life—that is, a life in full consciousness of our sensations, feelings, and thoughts.

A Few Guidelines

When you practice the therapy, you should remain in a secluded room, alone and, if possible, with a tape recorder at your disposal. Never simulate therapy or play "therapy games" with friends or relatives. All too often, what seems like understanding runs up against limitations.

A direct confrontation with parents and relatives on the subject of your past is fruitless unless those involved express an explicit desire to engage in such a dialogue. Before you decide to enter into one, you should think carefully about its worth. This is only relevant to those who are aware of the purpose and meaning of such a confrontation—namely, the achievement of positive personal change. Your therapy is "strictly private." An audience is not called for.

Leveling accusations at parents and guardians entails risks. Do so only in a secluded place. Because they lack a clearly defined intention, spontaneous confrontations often end disastrously. If you are nonetheless unable to refrain from engaging in an argument, remember that you are acting on your own initiative. The injury you may sustain could have been avoided.

Written Therapy

A written therapy is appropriate when material circumstances make "live" work impossible. Therapy by correspondence is a well-tried method for promoting self-help. Your situation, sensations, feelings, and conclusions can be very precisely formulated in written form, as can your needs and queries. Write as though you were speaking freely, without self-censorship. The four steps can be checked and supplemented in the act of rereading what you have written. A therapy based on writing and reflection cannot, however, be a complete substitute—at least not a reliable one—for the speaking/feeling part of the therapy that completes the therapeutic interaction.

For instance:

In the first step, Ruth describes a situation as follows: "Yesterday I was totally thrown by the presence of a particular colleague in my office. Robert has blue-gray eyes with black eyelashes and eyebrows . . . I don't know what makes me so confused when you are around. But you are clearly the reason. When you are there, everything else fades into the background. I watch every move I make. I feel self-conscious and confused."

The transition *to the second step* occurs without problem: "I always feel I have to please you. It unnerves me to be unable to act and think freely. I'm obsessed by knowing what you probably think of me. My need to be liked by you, to be taken notice of and accepted, overrides all other concerns in me. I am forever waiting for a sign that would tell me how much you are interested in me. The longer I have to wait, the more insecure I get. I can't think straight. I act artificially. When I see you next to me like now, I just want to cuddle up to you, gaze into your wonderful eyes, so deep and calm and dark, and find peace with you."

The third step begins with questions. For instance: "What prevents me from showing you I like you? Why do I feel so insecure when you are around? I don't even know how to behave anymore. It almost drives me out of my mind. I think that probably has to do with your girlfriend. You already have someone who belongs to you. I don't have a right to expect anything from you, and yet I do. I can hardly bear the fear of exposing myself and then being rejected. You're lucky. You have someone you belong to. You don't feel the need like I do to be loved and held and respected. It would hurt me terribly to see you make fun of me, laugh at me, because I want to be near you. More and more I feel like a little girl in your presence and act like one, too. I say things without thinking, things I then feel ashamed of afterward. You shake your head. What's happening with you? Is that you, Dad? Does the little girl in me still miss you? Is that still my unfulfilled need for my father, a person I can snuggle up to? Is that the child who longs for closeness, safety, security, and peace? Everything you never gave me? Have I become so insecure because I always had the feeling I wasn't allowed to be close to you? That you didn't like it? Didn't like *me?* I always tried to please you. But it was always in vain, just like now with Robby. I always had the impression that my trying bothered you. You never encouraged my interest in you, let alone reciprocated it. What made me insecure is that you never let me know that you liked me, liked me as I am."

The fourth step now becomes partially evident, when Ruth says, "I need *you* to tell me and make me feel that you think I'm smart and pretty and full of life and that you're proud of your daughter. One of my teachers once said that girls who are shown love grow up to be pretty. How I miss a father to love, one I am allowed to get close to, who caresses me, who I can be affectionate with and laugh with. (Now I'm beginning to feel sick, and there is a twitching in my back.)"

The interaction, steps one through four, begins again: "Dad, I always missed you, but I was never allowed to realize how much I needed you. Later I felt the distance between us, a kind of embarrassment on your part, when we did manage to talk. But I could never understand that. Once, when we talked together in the mountains, I felt as though we were closer. But you withdrew immediately, as though you were shy. Back then I was about twelve years old and bursting with enthusiasm to be able to get to know you and show you how very much we belonged together. My whole life you've never given me the chance to be really close to you. I was never able to learn how to really talk openly to you, how to be really honest with you; never allowed to show you my feelings, my fears, and my troubles. As soon as I felt I had finally established a footing with you, you always reacted in a strange way. You became awkward, embarrassed. You withdrew. Never was I allowed to show any deep feelings. Do I have to get sick for you to finally notice how much I need you, how desperate and hopeless my situation is? Why do you react to me like that? When I see you now in many different situations, I always have the same image before me. You are so strangely embarrassed, as though you were afraid of me. But I have never attacked you, have I? In fact, quite the opposite. I am always waiting for your attention so that I can show you how much you mean to me. Dad, I don't want to do anything bad to you. I don't want to seduce you. Is that what you're afraid of? Perhaps that's it—that *your own* sexuality makes you insecure, and that's why you always withdraw. But that doesn't have anything to do with me, you know. It's your problem that makes me feel unsure of myself. Why do you fancy me? Is it the girl who wants to love you who makes you so mixed up inside that you have to keep her at a distance for your own self-protection? But that's terrible. As your daughter, I can't make sense of that. I need to be able to feel totally at ease with you. I need to be able to experience myself as okay, to feel that I'm good and lovable and that I don't make men afraid of me. From a certain point onward I always felt uneasy at meal times, back then when my breasts began to show. You always looked at me in a sexual way. You laid down the law about what I should wear; otherwise people would be able to 'see all.' Recently, people have told me now and again that I have pretty eyes. But I always dismissed that as an empty compliment. But yesterday, after someone said that to me again, I looked in the mirror and realized my eyes weren't too bad after all. Lorenzo, my hairdresser, always tells me that there is something deep about my eyes, something that makes you want to plunge into them. Only recently have I begun to think that, maybe, I am not totally unattractive after all. Today, now that I am aware of my own sexuality, it disturbs me to feel that I'm not desirable and that I don't have any charisma. And I'm sure that's a consequence of my never having heard or felt any positive reinforcements from you, Dad. You never once told me I was lovable. The fact that you never gave me the feeling that I was as good as I was still hampers me today. I need that reinforcement from you, Dad. I need it, I have to hear it from *you,* because I love you, Daddy. Only then can I feel confident and self-assured. A nod of appreciation when I got good grades at school wasn't enough. I need to hear it, need to sense it, need to know that I am loved. Open your mouth for once, Dad. Say something friendly, something loving, something to make me feel more sure of myself and stop feeling so desperate about myself. Actually, I should feel desperate about you, about the brittle and distant way you have of relating to me. But, of course, I could not do that as a child. I'm certain there are tons of things wrong with me, probably just about everything. The way Mom nags at me only confirms my feelings of inadequacy. She is incapable of anything except criticism. And that's why I so desperately need your recognition, Dad."

Step by step, backward and forward. The important thing is to keep doing all four steps. The therapy may continue like this: "Why weren't you there for me? Why weren't you both able to give me that all-important feeling of security I needed from the start? Am I condemned to self-doubt my whole life long? Depressed and not knowing why? Always running after people, wearing myself out trying to please them, playing games to make them like me? But when they do, never being able to accept it, because you, my parents, never said it or made me feel it? It's not up to anyone else to help me. You're the ones who bear the responsibility. You should have been the ones to encourage me and help me to feel good about myself and the world. It was you who brought me into the world. I didn't have a choice. I am the continuation of your life. But I can't live up to that because you weren't there for me back then. If you had reinforced my sense of self, I wouldn't be so insecure, and at the same time so dependent on other people's opinions. It's not just that it's hard living like this. It's that so much energy goes into this fruitless search for recognition instead of being used for my own development. You didn't have the first idea what it meant to bring a child into the world, did you? I think you probably weren't even competent to do the job at all. Knowing you, you would probably say that it was God's will that I was born. But anyone can hide behind excuses like that, can't they? That way, any responsibility can be shunted off onto a higher authority. It's hard to believe, but there's no way around it—you actually didn't want to have anything to do with me. Sure, I had my uses—as a help around the house or to show off as a prize possession. But you don't seem to have had the first idea what I needed—either as a baby, or as a growing child or as an adolescent. What I needed to grow up to be a strong, healthy woman with both feet planted firmly on the ground; a woman who can defend herself and who knows what and who she is. Even today, I end up getting more used than loved, even by my boyfriend, though usually I am not even aware of it. I've become that accustomed to it. In my naïveté I mistake being used for being liked. In fact, the more I am used the more dependent I become. And if someone doesn't misuse me, I feel as though there is something wrong with *me*.

"Even though I am seeing this all for the first time, I still can't believe it. It's frightening what power you two have over my life. Sometimes I wonder how I can even relate to men at all. I have you, Johnny, my little brother, to thank for that. That was what "home" meant for me: sleeping in the same bed as Johnny. We shared a room until I was nine years old. I could always crawl into bed with him. He used to rub my back and comfort me. I've never again felt as safe and as happy as with him. I just start crying when I think about it. Johnny, it was never like that with anyone else, so quiet and peaceful. I never experienced that with you, Mom and Dad. That's why I was so jealous of any girl that smiled at you, Johnny. When you died everyone talked of you with respect. You were a cut above the rest. You were going to be a priest. Then, when you were only an altar boy, you were run over by a car on the way to church.

"What a state you must have been in that you weren't able to watch out for yourself. In my eyes you remained a rebel, someone I took off with on trips in my dreams. You are the one person I could come to at any time, could tell everything to. But now you're not there anymore. Can it be that the fear of losing you surfaces again and again in my relationships with men? Yes, now that has occurred to me, many things become clearer.

"You were three years older than I. I always feel like a sister to the men I am with. If I like a man, I always get into a melancholy mood. Until now I have never understood that. Inside, I am still your little sister, Johnny, the little sister who's looking for you everywhere but can't find you. I had to run away from home to find you and still I can't find you. Again and again I have been disappointed at not having found the support that you gave me as a child.

"How much humiliation, how much pain and suffering would I have been spared if you, you idiot parents, had given me what I so desperately needed to live!

A feeling of self-worth that would have allowed me to be as good to myself as Johnny was to me . . ."

Persons who have had severe psychic injury inflicted on them desperately need direct help. They also need comprehensive understanding from the therapist. They need to be able to lean on him and receive guidance. They need to be able to count on him. Their demands are neither insatiable nor boundless. But they need, in their desperation, an absolute commitment to their unique problems and personal history. Group therapy—as an extension of the basic therapy—can be of real help not only because there are others in the group who can also offer aid and guidance—naturally, the patient will seek guidance everywhere—but because in the same room other people are going through their own therapies, voicing their needs and standing up for themselves. One no longer feels all alone in the world with one's suffering. People who have given up all hope of finding their way back to life discover new energy and hope by seeing how even those with the severest psychic injuries can help themselves.

Group Therapy

The term simply describes the situation—a number of patients are in the same room and form a group. During therapy sessions in the primal group, personal contact or confrontation rarely takes place between participants. Each patient needs a reassuring "space" in which he or she can freely give voice to feelings and states of mind. Our groups are usually composed of three to five patients. Even "newcomers" quickly manage to find their feet within the group structure. Of course, it takes time until every participant is able to express himself without any self-censorship. The group constellation frequently provides powerful stimulus to the individual. For instance, the fact that the group may show itself to be deeply affected may be perceived as an attack. In this situation, every member of the group must realize that he is in therapy and that the stimulation provided by the others is to be viewed as the group's contribution to his own confrontation with his problems. Each member of the group must also literally have enough "space" for himself, so that at our center each participant has a space measuring five by seven feet, his or her private property, so to speak. The room is soundproofed with eight-inch-thick padding. The temperature is a constant 78 degrees F. The walls are painted a deep raspberry red to promote the feeling of lying in the womb. During the five-hour group sessions, the room is darkened. Each participant will find a flashlight at his place to help him orientate. Sanitary facilities, refrigerators, and the like are provided as a matter of course.

The primal process is continued within the group context. The therapy is pursued as practiced in the foundation therapy, but together with others. To be useful, stimuli provided by members of the group or by the therapists should be greeted with the necessary tolerance. Our goal is, in other words, supervised independence—to "do" our own therapy under professional supervision:

1. Express your state of mind and sensations.
2. Describe its effects: your feelings.

3. Question the consequences and persons involved, in order to
4. Formulate your own needs.

Vocal interjections can, of course, disrupt the group. The therapist will either make a separate room available to those with a need to scream for any length of time or ask the participant in question to look for another room. This particularly applies when the activity involves a direct release of pent-up energy. Of course, each participant is responsible and liable for his or her own actions, and everyone should first review the given circumstances to orient themselves within the group. This is not to say that a powerful outburst of rage cannot be of help to other participants.

Here, too, the therapy is best conducted with closed eyes. The therapist will help each member of the group in conformity with the initial agreement and to the extent that each situation requires.

Participants may submit therapy reports that the therapist will study. In addition, each member of the group can call the therapist in emergencies or ask him or her for additional information.

Each prospective group member signs a written statement pledging secrecy and respect for other participants. Should this pledge be violated, the consequence can be exclusion from the therapy. The right to take legal action is reserved.

The Group Context

In group therapy participants not only speak, complain, cry, rage, and, occasionally, laugh. They also register much past suffering. The group is the place where individual suffering finds a community and a context in which it can be worked through.

At the same time, each member of the group becomes aware of how uniquely personal his or her own history has been.

Even those who have been severely injured—persons suffering from psychoses—will find group work helpful. During a primal scene, they, like everyone else, should be able to feel safe. To do so, they usually require bodily contact. A hand or an arm is like a safety net protecting them from the plunge into the unknown. Without this kind of physical support, it would be too risky to enter into a truly devastating primal scene, such as those that underlie psychoses. The help provided by both group and therapist thus acts as a guarantor for the patient's protection. The therapist, the space, and the group serve as our map references as we embark on our fearful "journey into the jungle of the past" in search of recollections. The fragments with which we return help us to piece together the mosaic of our life and sufferings.

For instance: A woman wants to protest against the noise those around her are making. Suddenly she experiences a choking sensation and sees her mother's face, distorted with rage. The woman faints, to wake a short time later to report on what she has just experienced. She then talks about her thoughts and feelings regarding the abusive mother and intervenes on behalf of the child. A woman who has been so severely injured will usually need quite some time before being able to acknowledge her mother's demented behavior and react to it. All those who have been severely injured as children have latent psychotic reactions. These are measures taken in self-defense aimed at evading the reality of the abuse they suffered in the past. Had the child been capable of consciously experiencing such abuse, it would have either gone insane or died.

Psychoses are generalized, symbolized attempts to interpret and at the same time ward off a murderous past.

The fact that others are present in the group situation means that a patient who relives the experience of being raped is less likely to feel as though she has been raped here and now than if she was in a one-to-one session. Moreover, there are always others who have been through the same experience who can help with the work of integration. Violence in every form, but particularly sexual violence, requires extensive, in-depth work to enable the patient to completely resolve ever-recurrent guilt feelings.

The group situation can also be a place of surprise revelations. The laws governing our latent, unconscious reactions are invariably simple. It is the consequences that are extremely complex and hard to comprehend. Thus it may occur that an invisible connection suddenly becomes manifest in the light of another patient's remarks. For instance: A woman describes her reactions to sexual desire. As a rule she becomes dizzy and drowsy when she does so, dropping off into a kind of doze from which she awakens only after a brief rest. On the basis of her description of this reaction, she arrives, together with the therapist, at the following synopsis of her situation: although at first the patient is most capable of looking at a prospective partner and feeling good about an intimate encounter, as soon as she feels sexually aroused, she suffers an attack of vertigo and is forced to interrupt the situation and rest for a moment until she has regained possession of herself. In the course of describing the sequence of events, it becomes clear how her sensations and feelings evolve and where they lead. The woman chooses a partner she likes, looks forward to a developing intimacy, but is then blocked by a feeling of numbness as soon as she experiences arousal. In the past, she has sometimes even fainted, though this does not happen anymore. But the phenomenon continues to dismay and handicap her. The woman knows that she had a difficult birth, and this enables her to understand the process that takes place in her. She has a memory, dating back to the womb, of initial happiness—perhaps in anticipation of being freed from the constraint. This feeling of happiness entails a certain pleasure, perhaps the pleasure of movement, which leads to arousal. Unfortunately, the experience ended by no means pleasurably. The baby girl was brought into the world under "clinical conditions," i.e., the umbilical cord was cut too soon; she was slapped and her genitals pinched in order to "revive" her. The mother was unable to prevent this from happening. The physician attending her cynically ignored her pleas to cut the cord only after the blood had clearly ceased to flow and the pulsation had slowed. In addition, she was refused "rooming-in." As a result, the deeply frightened child did not receive sufficient comfort and consolation.

The adult woman—the former child—now realizes that her blackouts were a reaction to the arousal she sensed. They served the function of automatic "anesthesia," which set in as soon as arousal reached a certain level of intensity, spelling danger to her system in the form of anticipated pain. Thus, the woman discovered one of the most important latent reactions: loss of consciousness as a still-effective means of protection, allowing her to "survive" the torture that followed on her feelings of pleasure and happiness before the birth—a torture that in later life would be anticipated with fear. Loss of consciousness, developed in connection with feelings of pleasure and arousal, had become an autonomous reaction to ensure survival.

On hearing this, one of the members of the group reported having experienced the same phenomenon, albeit in another context. Every time he felt inspired by a scientific study that he would normally have read with pleasure, he became dulled and could not continue reading. After a few sentences, he would be overcome by dizziness and feel so close to fainting that he would have to lay aside the book and content himself with reading it sometime later. These two patients worked through the situation in therapy, and the symptoms subsequently disappeared.

The group thus provides many major and minor instances of assistance for one's own therapy. Sometimes it is only a small thing: for instance, one person becomes aware that he feels in some strange way compelled to arouse nearly everyone's animosity. Later he comes to see that he has had to do so to prevent any closeness developing with others—something he in reality wants, but is too frightened to establish. Other members of the group, witness to such revelations, can more easily recognize the structures underlying their own problems.

A Patient Writes

I have been asked to describe the therapy that I have recently begun.

J. Konrad Stettbacher's primal therapy is based on the premise that privation and overload in the earliest stages of life and in childhood are the foremost cause of psychic and organic afflictions. The fact that the child is totally dependent creates a situation in which it cannot (and may not) see and comprehend what is being done to it. Similarly, the child is not in a position to react appropriately to the mistreatment and disrespect it suffers. In fact, the child will also believe *itself* to be responsible for its own suffering.

The therapy helps me become aware of the privation and overload in my own past by letting me articulate my plight and demand of those who caused it why I was simultaneously subjected to, and deprived of, so much. I am able to express my fears and pain, my rage and indignation. I can see where I was mistreated and ask why. As a child I was never allowed to do all of this out of fear of my parents and so had forgotten it. Later, I was no longer able to ask the questions that could have helped me understand why I am as I am.

My parents' rejection and disregard for me implanted itself so deeply in me that I no longer understood anything. Every day was a torture of unbearable emotions. I felt I was always in the way—superfluous, useless, inept, and, above all, guilty and bad. The effort put into out-maneuvering or evading these feelings left me exhausted. At times I felt like committing suicide, to finally do what my parents had not had the courage to do, although deep inside it was what they had all along wanted—to "abort" myself.

Because I was constantly plagued by feelings of being useless and guilty, I no longer felt I had any right to exist. Every day I had to struggle to prove to myself that I was living for "something." Again and again I went through the experience of not being good enough to be really loved by someone else. No amount of self-sacrifice or help for others, no amount of begging and desperate trying was enough to make me feel I was truly valuable and loved.

With the therapy, I am now gradually coming to realize what effects my parents' power over me during childhood and youth has had on me. I realize that I am the only one who can help me. To do so I must become aware, both intellectually and emotionally, of all the destructive and negative aspects of my childhood. I have to confront just how much that hurt me—and still hurts when something or someone reminds me of it.

With the help of this therapy, I am gradually freeing myself from the compulsion to confuse others with my parents in an emotional sense. Before, I kept trying to find in others the parents I never had. In order not to feel it, I was forced to repress the pain.

The therapist teaches me how to become the "child's advocate" and supports me in that process. I am steadily becoming more capable of giving voice to my feelings—of yelling out my protest; dissolving my sorrow in tears; putting my anger into words. These days I am increasingly able to make the connection between my difficulties and distress and the underlying causes.

Step by step, I am leaving behind my negative expectations and compulsions and am now confident that I will ultimately be able to completely free myself from these unreal restraints.

Proofs of the positive changes in my life are already there. Recently I have been able to look people in the eye and speak to them without fear. It is no longer difficult for me to be able to do without cigarettes and alcohol. I can laugh again.

The Therapist Writes

Dear Patient,

I would like to set down a few more thoughts on the therapy that will perhaps help you to reach your goal.

The aim of our therapy can be summed up, in simplified form, in one sentence: we want to become what we are in order to live as we like.

Of course, that is easier said than done. Become what we are? But we are what we are! Of course. But we are no longer able to know and feel much of what we are. We have long ago "forgotten" the angry, tight-lipped, suffering, and desperate child within us who was totally at the mercy of his elders. We have an aversion to everything from the past that troubles and pains us, and we fight against it with all our might. Getting through each new day is hard enough. By necessity, we underestimate the power the past exerts over us and battle our way through the present.

Now you have decided to unravel the past step by step. You want to—and you will—find out who and what caused your physical and mental suffering. You can successfully learn to rid yourself of "that." But you will be obstructed in your search by a widely held opinion, namely: "My parents and their generation were kind, well-meaning, and upright people. Surely they can't have been responsible for my suffering." To some extent, this may be true. But it doesn't alter the fact of your suffering and the restrictions that were placed on your life.

In my opinion, we are only fully capable of living when our primal integrity has been respected in such a way that our knowledge of what we need has not been impaired. If our capacity to feel and sense remains intact, we will always know what we need to be, and remain, healthy.

That means the older generation had not, as a rule, yet understood what we need to be healthy. Your parents did not know what you needed as a child. The child's needs—your needs—were not given sufficient consideration. That neglect is what caused your suffering.

Now you want to take up the trail of your injuries and helplessness as a child and resolve them. Bear in mind, this is a major undertaking that will require a great deal of time. You will have to strive to stop suppressing the pain and instead face and resolve that which causes it. The point is not to tolerate and endure pain and fear. In therapy, you will learn how to react when they arise so that, with time, they will resolve themselves.

What changes can you expect?

You will be able to feel again your natural needs.

You will try to fulfill them and no longer have to pursue substitute needs. Inappropriate defense reactions will disappear. You will no longer be enslaved to tormenting phantoms. You will be able to organize your life in accordance with your potential and in such a way that it contributes to your sense of well-being.

I wish you luck and all the energy you will need in this endeavor. I also hope that during the work you have time to catch your breath. The healing process, like any other natural process, takes its time.

J. Konrad Stettbacher

How You Were Born . . .

How you were born is how you will live. If you were really wanted by your mother and father, you will be able to love. You will want to live and take pleasure in living. If you were really respected by your mother and father, you will respect life.

It doesn't, though, do us much good to complain about "the drama of the ungifted mother" or to shout: "I've had it with being a pathogenic factor. We mothers are fighting back. We refuse to be placed on a pedestal by the rest of mankind. We're not some kind of filter between the dirty, wicked world and the good, clean family. We refuse to go on listening to the accusations of so-called experts and their contradictory advice. They all just serve one purpose—to make mothers feel guilty."

It is equally senseless and dangerous to claim that mothers are responsible for asthma, drug addiction, and impotence. Even if that were the case, to simply blame mothers would be pointless. What is needed is insight and comprehension. To label mothers as "guilty" merely recreates the myth of Eve. No one on earth would knowingly let such a burden of guilt mount up, like a debt that can never be repaid or worked off, and that even our creditors can never hope to recover. If we didn't learn to manage the economy of our lives better, such a burden of psychological debt would simply annihilate us. One thing alone remains to us—to admit our guilt, acknowledge our ignorance, and show our remorse to the person we have wronged.

Many parents consciously or unconsciously deny their guilt toward their children—to the detriment of everyone concerned and society at large. I believe nearly every child would be willing to freely forgive its parents for even grave mistakes if only the parents showed themselves willing to cooperate in bringing about a reconciliation. Unfortunately, many parents insist on their infallibility and categorically reject any responsibility for their children's illness or misfortune. In therapy, this attitude again and again blocks and hinders the desired healing. It can even prevent it entirely. The fact that parents deny any responsibility for their guilty behavior, thereby deceiving their children, is often the real cause of their children's suffering. The parents' denial makes the child feel confused and guilty. The hypocritical assurance that they genuinely wanted the child is, by its nature, a heavy burden to bear. It further imprisons the child in its apparent guilt. Every father and mother who have damaged a child psychologically can do the child no better service than to strive to understand their own mistakes in order to relieve it of its confusion and doubt.

Simple admissions of guilt are, however, of no help to anyone. Blunt "confessions" to the child that it was conceived by mistake, that it was an "accident," merely confirm the parents' underlying brutality. Even if they feel they have good reason to do so, parents don't have the right to behave unjustly and aggressively toward their children. If they do so, then it is because of internal or external circumstances *in their own lives* for which the child is not responsible. Parents who have made mistakes have a duty to apologize to their children. *"I can't live if you don't want me and cannot love me"* is the inevitable refrain of every unwanted, and therefore unloved, child. Thankfully, children do occasionally find someone outside their immediate family circle who will love them. But judging by the state of many people's lives and their desperation, it does not happen often. There can be no reason whatsoever to consciously bring children into the world without loving them—unless the motives are egotism, exploitation, or contempt for mankind. Yet day after day, a thousand times over, this happens blindly. The result is a daily increase in destructive potential, a daily increase in people assisting in the collapse of our world—people who have been conceived blindly and irresponsibly and who do little except destroy themselves or the environment. Man, who was in prehistoric times a shy, unobtrusive animal, has become "the Lord of Creation." As such, he is *the* responsible form of life on the planet. We must all soon learn to live up to that responsibility if we are to put a stop to the destruction of life.

This is why responsibility for the whole begins with the individual. The individual, however, can only assume this charge if he is conscious of himself and his environment. And this means, above all, parents. *They* can examine and question their motives and their behavior. A child can only do so in time and if its integrity has remained intact. People who have not been allowed to become conscious in this sense and, as a result, have injured or damaged their children, have a hard time coming to terms with their guilt. Without outside help, they will do their utmost to avoid having to acknowledge the sad consequences of their behavior.

In a culture where responsibility is constantly being delegated to those "higher up," the denial of guilt is the rule. Guilt does not necessarily just mean that we have committed criminal deeds. In German, the word *Schuld* has a double meaning: "debt" and "guilt." And by guilt, I mean above all the sense of remaining indebted, of owing something, of not having been able to care enough or give enough—in other words, of *not* having acted, strictly speaking. Objectively speaking, only the child can be "owed" something because it is in a state of need and dependency. For a child to be indebted to someone who is, from the very beginning, effectively "omnipotent"—bigger, stronger, richer, more experienced and knowledgable—is clearly utterly illogical. Only those with power can become indebted—and, in this sense, "guilty"—to those who are powerless. What can a small child, however furious it is, do to its father? Parents don't need to demand obedience. Children are quick to learn. If parents are able to set an example in their own lives, their children will automatically imitate the good.

Today, "everything" bears down on us. And because we no longer grow up in the security of small, closed groups, the security afforded by the family unit is all the more important. A protected, secure childhood is the essential foundation for a human being to attain consciousness. The child who learns to communicate without fear will be able to perceive many things and interrelationships. It will be able to comprehend the world in all its different facets.

The most influential and stimulating event in our lives is our birth. Almost nothing else in the entire course of our lives can engender such a comprehensive, cataclysmic stimulation of the senses as this. It will be the benchmark for all later sensory stimulation. Any kind of stimulation will activate the memory of our birth. Stimulation is a consequence of excitation—both an alarm response and/or a mobilization effect that influences the entire organism. Stimulation is accompanied by a total psychic and emotional attentiveness and by events requiring actions and reactions. For the space of nine months, we are "in paradise." There, undisturbed and in protected dialogue with our mother, our organism forms itself out of the building blocks of millennia of evolution. At the end of our term in paradise, the pressure upon us gradually begins to mount. We want release from constriction, and we marshall our forces in response to this need. Prior to this release, there is a perceptible sense of joy and pleasure, something that I can recall and that others who have traced their memories this far back can also remember in detail. The sensory stimulation that sets in is a result of the extreme physical exertion and activity required for the approaching event. This in turn should be something pleasurable if the flexing, massagelike motions of the birth are allowed to be experienced in their completeness. To be born with a sense of physical pleasure, with joy and a feeling of safety and being welcome, would be the most desirable way to begin one's life. Yet all too often this beginning is little more than a brutal, painful expulsion from paradise. Sometimes it is deliverance from hell into the torture chamber of the delivery room. Here, a living being is "unwittingly" tortured, a being who should in later life be capable of finding its way in life. The child's unconscious, though, will never forget being thus expelled and cast out. Before being freed from its constriction, it had sensed joy and pleasure. This, you could say, was its state of being at the dawn of experience. When birth, accompanied as it is by extreme stimulation, ends as an agony of torture, the infant's phylogenetic repertoire—its inherited memories—will be unable to find any equivalence for this experience. It does not yet have at its disposal any terms under which it can classify and comprehend this monstrous experience. The infant feels itself mistreated, pushed and pulled about, squashed, beaten, hung up by its heels, choked and strangled—and this, by strange, alien powers. The only way of surviving this ordeal is by means of the body's built-in capacity to become numb. If the organism did not have this safety valve, the overload of the pain would damage the organs and even cause death. Lapsing into unconsciousness does not, however, prevent the body from storing this "data"—which is crucial to its survival—in the unconscious. Thus even peripheral events before and after the blackout are recorded in detail, to wait on recognition and interpretation at a later date. The tormented little being will, in the meantime, register the outlines of things and people that will later become vehicles for the recollection of the event. If we later work through our memories, this stored information will become of use. If not, it will become the stuff of bad dreams haunting us by night and causing confusion by day. It may even cause us physical damage. Once our bodies have registered these horrendous traumatizations, it is not surprising that the experience becomes for us the epitome of hell, banned to the unconscious as the terror of all terrors, stored as a warning of mortal agony.

Imagine a doctor yanking an infant out of its crib by the feet, holding it upside down and slapping it. Even in our culture, such a person would be regarded as crazy and a public menace. But a few days earlier, at a birth, such behavior is sanctioned by medical practice. And this, at a moment when the child's central nervous system is at its most sensitive and educable. In a sense, we become more and more forgetful from the moment of our birth onward as we are forced to absorb and process an ever-increasing number of impressions. A newborn baby has had no experience whatsoever of the world other than that of being in the womb. How amazing, then, that so little care and protection is shown toward an infant being at the time of greatest sensitivity and vulnerability.

Every instance of sensory stimulation in our lives will elicit an echo of the brutality of our births and exert a corresponding influence on all our actions without our being aware of it. Does that mean torture is the basis of life? Sadly, the answer is, all too often, yes. The latent reactions, burdens, and handicaps to which this torture gives rise, different as they may be for each of us, will have the same disruptive influence on the rest of our lives.

How can we live a normal, autonomous life when our lives began with such a psychic overload? The answer is, we won't. We will suffer, labeled as neurotic or psychopathic or some other aberration, because no one has the desire or the ability to understand what has happened to us. Everything we do will be dangerous. Exertions will be messengers of doom that almost plunge us into unconsciousness. We will not love life. We will endure it, unable to come to terms with ourselves or the world. Everything we do will be an agony. Our world will be overshadowed by anxiety, our lives tyrannized by fear.

Each birth has different consequences. It can become a lifelong support, the foundation of our primal trust—or it can disfigure every day of our lives.

Latent negative reactions arise from a multiplicity of psychic overloads. Anything connected with pleasure, for instance, may elicit anxiety or fear. The experience of stasis in the womb gives rise to a latent feeling of being locked up or locked in and leads to avoidance, or even refusal, the moment pleasure in motion is registered. The experience of numbness during birth produces a tendency to "play dead" or become stiff and motionless. It can also lead to a feeling of suffocation, especially when we are confronted by danger. The experience that becoming numb is *the* way to cope with the unbearable will promote or cause narcolepsy (the compulsion to sleep). The search for an anesthetic will often lead, in later life, to smoking—a probative narcotic and, at the same time, a means of dealing with stress. The prolonged pain resulting from a complicated delivery or the negligence and insensitivity of those attending a birth—all sheer torture to the infant—will result in corresponding periods of anesthetization lasting for months, years, or even decades. Pain suffered in the womb or during birth, which involves paralysis and numbness, will result in a loss of sensation. It can even lead to paresis (paralysis, weakening of a muscle or group of muscles) as in symptoms of morphologically determinable damage to the cerebral substance, i.e., the functional reactions of infantile cerebral palsy. In my opinion, one of these fatal latent reactions is multiple sclerosis. For those who suffer from this disease every spontaneous action or reactive pleasure, every creative urge or desire for movement, instantaneously triggers the warning: "Be careful! Don't do it! It could be dangerous!" Furthermore, the latent readiness to counter danger makes complete mental and physical relaxation impossible.

Overloads of pain, feelings of torture and being left alone before, during, and after birth will permanently impair our ability to lead a fulfilled life and detract from our pleasure at being alive.

In light of the terrible "fate" awaiting the victims of ignorance, one hardly dares to enumerate the many problems caused by suffering, suffering that is not inevitable. Forethought could make it avoidable. There are those who manage to make a virtue out of suffering. Perhaps this is of help, and provides a reason for living to a badly disturbed person. But it is a poor and bitter substitute for a fulfilled life. The child, the human being, gives expression to its desperation night and day. Here lies the parents' chance to help their children.

It is possible to heal even severe psychic injuries provided that parents respond to the child's appeals for help, its signals. Every time the child is consoled or its needs genuinely satisfied, its agitation will be quieted. Loving physical care and the affirmation that this little creature is worthy of respect and love will heal almost any wound. Injuries, insecurities, and confusions can be reversed with words and deeds once they have been recognized as such. The mentally deaf can learn to hear, the mentally mute can learn to speak, the mentally blind to see.

Healing usually requires a great deal of time, persistence, and patience. But the joys of progress will be ample reward for the effort. Bear in mind, the overloaded child will for a long time be unable to express satisfaction or joy. In the beginning, it will require much energy to satisfy the child. It will be highly sensitive and easily upset. It will often express fear and give the impression that its needs are insatiable. The child will not immediately be able to trust the "new order" as it has already erected a system of defenses that will not be dropped overnight. It needs sensitive parents who can maintain their care and attention until it can regain its sense of trust.

Sadly, many parents never notice their child's distress and are unwilling to take a critical look at themselves in order to help it. Instead, "the problem" is delegated to experts who, more often than not, have no idea of the real afflictions and their underlying causes. One of the reasons for this is that parents never fully inform them of the details. Immediate help is the most reliable safeguard against chronic suffering. Mothers who are able to nurse and comfort their infants after a difficult birth and give continual encouragement can prevent lasting damage. Damage can also be "repaired" if parents treat their children with the care and love they need. After enduring such pain, a child needs healing care and affection for body and soul. For her part, the mother needs support from others and an inner stability that enables her to be emotionally there for the child.

The inability to feel pleasure in the act of breast-feeding seems to be a widespread problem. Sometimes mothers have problems with breast-feeding because of "moral scruples" or because they have trouble relating to their own bodies. Healthy mothers feel pleasure throughout their bodies when they breast-feed, particularly in the breasts and genital region. This is, if you like, Nature's way of rewarding the mother for providing primal nourishment. Breast-feeding can be the most intensive, pleasurable act of communication between mother and child. In addition to providing all the antibodies and nutrients the infant needs, the act of sucking from the breast also pleasurably stimulates the infant's organs and functions. This in turn paves the way for establishing satisfying relationships in later life. Pleasurable and satisfying breast-feeding is a first-rate foundation for positive psychosocial development. This stimulating, life-giving contact with the mother instills in the child a positive sense of identity and a stable foundation for its feeling of self-worth as a living being. A child whose needs are fully satisfied will strive to live a rich, fulfilling existence and share this pleasure with others.

To be capable of being "life-givers," mothers need the support of fathers and society's recognition. We cannot, and do not want, to do without "real" mothers. Test-tube babies have already been characterized as "monsters," and it is inconceivable that they could produce anything but "monsters" in their turn. To me, it seems a lot more sensible to prevent unconscious people from creating "monsters" than to await the development of artificial means of reproduction. And I am convinced that we will manage to evolve into conscious human beings. We don't have any other choice. It is our only chance of survival.

Needs and Perversions

Before the discovery of the fertility cycle, sexuality and its inevitable consequence, unwanted pregnancy, were profound problems for mankind. Despite the many birth-control methods available today, this is still the case. What makes us, then, produce unwanted offspring?

Our reproductive urges are regulated by our bodies' hormones. Is this a compulsion? A legacy of nature? Or is it that something in us wants to escape? To no longer be driven? Do we want to be comforted or experience pleasure? Is sexuality the way we release tension or pass on life? Do we want to preserve the species? Perhaps it is all this, and more?

Today, everyone who is fertile should be conscious of what he or she wants from a sexual encounter. Is it an erotic adventure? Or the desire to conceive a child in love? If the aim is to have a child, then this should be done in full knowledge of the responsibility for the new life we are creating. It is a crime to conceive a child in ignorance or as a plaything. Unfortunately, sexuality often serves as an arena for acting out our latent reactions—as an enjoyable way of abusing power; as an expression of contempt or the sadistic pleasure of causing pain. The pretense of love, as a pretext for using sex to abreact, is probably the most common form of abuse.

Children experience pleasurable sensations in the genital region without it necessarily being "sexual" before they reach puberty. The word *sexuality* should be used to mean the act of procreation and the copulation urge. Clearly, children do not want to engage in the act of procreation. They are not capable of reproduction. When children have an erect penis or clitoris, it in no sense indicates a desire for sexual intercourse. Rather, it signals a general arousal without specific cause. This can be either pleasurable or painful when the respective part of the body is engorged with blood. The number 6, meaning sex, is a sign of arousal, a symbol. The penis has often been observed to become erect both when a man dies a natural death and at an execution. Death can be an extremely stimulating, agitating event. Any arousal, regardless of the incident that prompts it, can be easily "released" by overstimulation of the erect penis or clitoris. This will localize the increase in stimulation until a climax is achieved. The built-up tension then rapidly subsides as it is dispersed throughout the entire body. We experience this as an orgasm and immediately "go slack." At the same time, a wave of relaxation flows through us. Our central nervous system registers the event thus: "The deed is done, the danger has passed." Now, the organism can temporarily demobilize and rest.

Arousal is a consequence of excitation. It is an

alarm or mobilization signal in the organism. Arousal always affects all the body's organs, particularly those with key survival functions. These organs are also especially sensitive to pain, e.g., the female ovaries or male testicles. Anxiety attacks in the form of cramps in a girl's or woman's lower abdomen can cause a sympathetic reaction in the ovaries so acute that even today the word *hysteria*—derived from the Greek *hystera*, meaning "uterus"—is used to describe the resultant expressions of pain, even though the uterus has virtually nothing to do with it. "History" would be a much better term in that it would make clear to the person suffering that the cause is to be found in her own life story. Pain is caused by tension that sets in because we are unable to consciously experience arousal. Instead, we feel bound to suppress it in response to an unconscious warning of danger. When expressions of arousal are suppressed, both children and adults can sometimes experience pain in the head, back, and pelvic area, along the stimulus conductor of the spinal cord. Assuming it isn't prevented from doing so, a child can find relief by making rocking motions starting from the pelvis before the cramps set in. This self-help method, which closely resembles the motions of birth or mating, can ward off the pain of cramps or spasms. A more intense means of combating an arousal signaling the anticipation of fear or pain is manual overstimulation of the genitals.

Clearly, in certain instances "sexual behavior" has virtually nothing to do with sexuality. A child who is rocking himself or masturbating cannot be described as "sexual." Sadly, adults use this label time and again to justify sexually abusing children. Child sexual abuse is a serious crime with lifelong consequences for the victim. Even if the victim is ignorant of what has happened, cannot articulate it, or has attempted to make a "virtue" of the incident, he or she will remain in a state of suffering.

Every instance of arousal evokes echoes of all past events or incidents that accompany arousal. The quality of those past experiences will largely determine how we are able to perceive our present arousal. Whether we are "one with ourselves" and therefore able to enjoy the stimulation or whether we immediately panic depends on what our past experience has been. *One* experience, above all others, will be crucial and exert the profoundest influence on our lives—the birth experience. It constitutes the most far-reaching state of arousal we will have ever experienced. The more positive and strengthening was our birth, the more capable we will be of experiencing arousal and hence sexuality as a free, satisfying, and enjoyable experience. Conversely, the more painful and stressful the birth, the more urgent and compulsive will be the need to abreact and annul arousal. In the context of sexuality, this can lead to disorders manifested as perversions or impotence. In the same way it can lead to compulsive, unconscious sex, which not only leaves the partners unsatisfied but also results in unwanted pregnancies. The search for the comfort, security, and shelter we ourselves never had is often the motive behind unwanted pregnancies. The unconscious compulsion to escape from the imminent pain and disaster (the birth) that the state of arousal announces overrides all reason.

It is therefore hard to escape the alarming conclusion that the unconscious attempt to escape the agony of birth often leads, in later life, to the production of unwanted children. In this way, the most important human urge, namely the urge to reproduce, without which the human race could not continue, becomes confused with painful experiences and transformed into perversion.

As the example of sexuality proves, every natural human need can be perverted, degenerate, and cause suffering. The basic mechanism is always the same: the danger of perversion arises when primal needs are abused or neglected, causing pain and anxiety that the child cannot integrate. The victim has no alternative but to circumvent these inner threats. Either he will avoid sexuality altogether or he will live out his sexuality in a perverted manner. In the process, he is incapable of realizing that the perversion (i.e., the degenerated need) is a defensive reaction designed to avoid pain and deception. And the more the perversion finds legitimation as a natural need, the more our natural needs will be submerged.

If the hurt child's feelings could speak, they would say something like this: "I won't let you love me. Don't try and tell me you love me. I've known for a long time that I am unlovable. No way will I let myself fall for your/my feelings. That would be fatal. Loving is a sickness that has to be countered with deception, rejection, shame, and pain. I know what the score is. All this dumb talk about being loving and supportive—love is just about manipulating people. I am never again going to fall for those lies.

"You mean there's someone out there who really understands a child? Who supports it and is willing to stand up for it? No strings attached? I don't believe it.

"I've had enough disappointment. My life-insurance policy is to trust no one."

The child who has been subjected to continuous abuse no longer allows itself to feel its own natural needs. To do so would be too dangerous and too painful. The hurt child is frightened. Pain and anxiety threaten it. To escape its oppressive memories and expectations, it effectively renounces its own naturalness.

The memory of sexual traumas is extremely problematic. Such experiences will be neatly repressed and dismissed by the victim as sick fantasies. At the same time, every victim will fight against the memory out of fear that he or she was to blame for the experience, thinking: "If I hadn't wanted it to happen to me, it never would have." But provided they are all reported, the symptoms will immediately indicate sexual injury to an experienced therapist.

All sexual perversions are the offspring of injuries committed to a child's integrity. To concentrate solely on pinpointing sexual events will, however, obstruct the therapeutic process. It takes time for a person to be able to realize—and bear—the "naked truth." The direct results of sexual abuse, such as frigidity, perversion, or psychosis, cannot be resolved by simply retrieving the respective memory. First, the therapeutic work must be accomplished. One special difficulty involved in resolving such afflictions is that the degree of arousal during sexual experiences is, by definition, very high. And this blurs the distinction between sexual arousal and pain. In other words, the difference between the two will often not be perceived. The chain of reactions—arousal-overstimulation-relaxation—circumvents multiple instances of pain charged with sensations and feelings, including serious anxieties. Pain is often simply accepted as part of the price of sexuality's dynamic states of arousal. The main concern is: "The deed is done, the danger has passed."

Openness and honesty are preconditions of any therapeutic help. If a patient chooses to hide his plight out of shame or embarrassment and opts instead to hurt himself—or allow himself to be hurt—in order to avoid the old physical and psychic pain, he is incapable of allowing himself to be helped. Men and women who have suffered oral, genital, or anal sexual abuse as children have the tendency to seek overstimulation and pain. In this way they prevent memories from surfacing and seek to evade their primal pain. These "cover-up" strategies afford temporary relief. Ultimately, they become like an addiction, facilitating further injuries that serve to cement the affliction. Manipulation with objects, perversions, obsessive sexuality, and prostitution are always aftereffects of multiple injuries to a child's body and soul. The suffering can only be healed if we are fully committed to the process.

Perversions serve the purpose of circumventing the physical or psychic pain that arises as soon as a natural need is felt. In addition, perversions have the function of covering up anxiety and pain stemming from traumatic experiences and keeping them unrecognizable.

Criminality

In 1959, the General Assembly of the United Nations adopted the Declaration of Children's Rights. Were it to be enforced, this ten-part declaration would successfully banish all types of criminal behavior relating to children. But thirty years after their proclamation, children's rights are seldom mentioned, still less enforced. Biographies of criminals, when they are thorough, give us plenty of information on the origins of criminal behavior. If one knows that the child's integrity was injured and its needs neglected, it is not difficult to spot the reasons (triggers) for the subsequent crimes in a criminal's childhood. If a person has exhibited criminal behavior and wishes to free himself of this compulsion, he must examine and work through his own past. He must undergo therapy and in so doing resolve the destructive urges that were inculcated during childhood as apparent solutions to his personal plight.

So, does criminality, like perversion, have its roots in unsatisfied needs?

The answer is yes. As a rule, it stems from a denial of responsibility. As the child never learns what its rights are, how can it demand them? If neither the parents nor the community assumes responsibility for these rights, it will grow up partially or wholly dispossessed of them. Every child has the right to be protected and cared for, particularly as children are never asked if they wish to be brought into the world or not. Social competence, the essential quality for the survival of human society, grows from a child's positive experience and its being able to see that its role models assume their responsibility toward it and the environment. A child whose needs have been satisfied will turn into a socially competent human being capable of contributing constructively to the community.

A child's paramount need is to be respected. Every child who is shown attention and respect will be able to articulate all its other needs and has a good chance of having them satisfied. Even if the child's needs for nourishment, education, and the like are not all fully met, it will be able to ask for more and will not be turned away or put off with excuses. Children who are respected can find their way in the world. They will show respect for the needs of others. Such children do not commit self-serving crimes or take revenge for *supposed* injustices. Instead, they will protect the right to life and the right to have their natural needs satisfied.

Criminality is a perversion of the need for respect. Perverted behavior toward society, others, and life in general is the result of nonrespect. If parents fail to respect and satisfy their children's needs, their sons and daughters will later transfer their claim to other people and institutions. Using violence or manipulation they will attempt to force the world at large to respect and satisfy their, by now perverted, needs. Often enough, however, criminal behavior will be held up as admirable, intelligent human conduct, a smart strategy in life's battle to survive. It is the upstart's claim to the rights of the strong, cunning, and intelligent, those who supposedly have the right to take whatever they can and do whatever they want. The risk of being caught or killed in the process is just an occupational hazard. "He lived life to the full and made the most of what he had," people will say of the criminal. The damage he caused will soon be forgotten. Children who are led down the path of criminality cannot be happy. No matter what they end up specializing in, be it business, politics, academia, or syndicated crime, they will always do damage to others. Unfortunately, criminality knows no boundaries. It exists in all professions.

Criminality is the perversion of respect for the lives and needs of others. It is an irresponsible disregard and contempt for other persons and their property.

The Enemies of Life

How sad, to have only enemies and no friends. Can it really be so? Is life simply about struggle? Or is the maxim "Life is a battle for survival" a distortion of Darwin? Researchers claim that the adaptability of a species is an essential criterion for natural selection. Do we human beings really have such difficulties adapting? Looking around us, it is hard to believe. Technology has even enabled us to adapt to conditions on the moon. So how is it that on this planet people are daily killed, murdered, and tortured, usually at the behest of some "higher authority"? Victims and enemies alike are labeled as "evil" or "dangerous" and condemned to annihilation without further justification. Are these just mercenary deeds that any of us could have committed as long as somebody else takes responsibility and picks up the tab? Or are there specific reasons for such acts? Certainly, there seem to be as many reasons to kill others as there are people on the planet. But luckily not everyone has a life story that "outfits" them to kill without qualms on someone else's orders. People with other kinds of personal histories have no desire to kill even if they are ordered to. They even balk at killing in self-defense.

So what makes a killer?

A longing for death and pleasure in killing are caused by a hostility to life inculcated in childhood. Life, for a child like this, has been such an ordeal that it can hardly wait to live out its hatred of life and take revenge for having been made to live the unlivable. Under normal circumstances, the person's own fear and pain act as a brake, but if they get their hands on power anything is possible. The deeds of mass murderers like Stalin, Hitler, or Ceausescu are common knowledge. Much less is known about the origins of their destructiveness. At least, there is little discussion on the subject. Yet to know how these men became monsters would be invaluable if we are to learn how to prevent such catastrophes, and the suffering they bring with them, from occurring in the future. Of course, concerning ourselves with such monsters is not pleasant—particularly if it involves confronting the "monster" in ourselves. Since so many inhabitants of our planet have been maltreated at the beginning of their lives, there lives in many of us a tormenting spirit of proportionate size. Like the genie in the bottle, if the monster within is so big that, when it expands, it threatens to shatter the glass, things can get dangerous. We will pose a latent danger not only to ourselves but to others. To prevent this genie of destruction escaping and developing into a horrendous monster, we have to keep the cork tightly in place.

The raging despair of abused children is blindly directed against everything and everyone. "I was so angry I felt like destroying the whole world" is a confession one often hears from abused persons. Words like "seething with rage" or "mad enough to kill" are too weak to describe the feelings of someone who longs for death and hates to live. If a person is unable to resolve the murderous hatred generated in the first few years of his life, he will transfer this hatred to everyone with whom he comes in contact. Alternately, he will himself become the victim by developing a destructive illness, ending as a sacrificial lamb on the altar of his parents. After all, "The only good child is a dead child." The unconscious wish to die shapes more lives than one might think.

"The Murderers Are Among Us" is not just a film title. It is day-to-day reality. Murderers are "made" and then set loose on the human race. Those who raise children to become latent murderers must despise mankind.

The Guardians of Life

"Feelings and sensations aren't so important. It's best to forget them as quickly as you can." A person who thinks like this is a child of the times. We live in an age in which intellectual virtuosity and dazzling intelligence are showered with respect and rewards. What usually gets overlooked is the fact that, in evolutionary terms, it is only relatively recently that the intellect has been raised to such a pinnacle of importance. For millions of years before that it was feeling and sensation that guided and directed life. Without these faculties, life would have been, and remains, impossible. They are the guardians of our species, of life itself. As such, they are the most valuable asset we possess. These two "authorities" constantly watch over and influence us, even in our sleep. If we heed them, they keep us on track about every aspect of our lives—the past, the present, and the future; what is good for us and what is not. It is essential that we listen to these "guardians of life," that we don't ignore or neglect them—that we remain "open" to them. In the early stages of our lives, our sensations and feelings are especially strong and alert. We must therefore strive to keep them that way. We must see to it that our guardians do not become numb or dulled. If they become mute or debilitated, deaf or drunken, they are of no use to us. In this way, it is crucial that we do not mislead children into ignoring these faculties that Nature has been developing in us for millennia. Becoming fully conscious, and remaining so, means listening to our natural, primal feelings and sensations and allowing ourselves to be guided by them. We must rediscover a sense of our own modest place in Nature. We must learn to respect Nature and cherish the help she offers. These are the tidings of the times.

Each child comes into the world with its very own guardians. It is up to its parents and society to keep them healthy so that they can give it life-long support and help. In other words: a child needs *love*. Love is not a thing. Love is life. It means being alive and caring for life. Life creates needs. To fulfill them is to fulfill love. Love sustains life. All a child wants is to be loved.

For Your Information

If, having read the description of the therapy, it appeals to you, you can use the text as a set of guidelines for self-help. For this you will need a secluded room, time, patience, and a tape recorder to enable you to review your sessions. The therapy always begins with your present state of mind, your problems, thoughts, and feelings—in other words, with what is most pressing here and now. The book offers a means to learn the therapy and supervise its course.

People seeking help often ask if there are risks and dangers involved in the therapy. We grown-up children are terribly fearful, aren't we? But what do we really fear? The risks of therapy? I don't think so. Far more it is our own distant past, the awfulness of which can never be matched, that strikes fear into our souls.

Does the therapy entail dangers? One possible danger could be working with an unsuitable therapist who might overburden or mislead a patient in the process of uncovering the truth. A competent therapist, on the other hand, is an invaluable help. If the therapy has to be conducted independently, without the active supervision of a therapist, few risks are involved. For someone who has a grasp of evolution and who has thoroughly acquainted themselves with the book *Making Sense of Suffering,* the danger of "losing oneself," i.e., of losing one's intellectually controlled consciousness, is minimal. A valuable prerequisite for therapy is the study of the works of Alice Miller.

Assuming that the therapy is not affected by any external dangers or disturbances and that the patient is not placed under excessive strain, the one possible danger is that the patient may abandon the therapy halfway through and thus abandon himself. This is especially dangerous when the therapy releases acute physical—and sometimes psychic—pain. This pain and fear would, of course, occur even without therapy but could be combated or "treated" as a physiological or psychological abnormality.

"Informed" opinion has it that when acute physical pain does occur, it can *only* be due to organic, and not psychological, damage. As a result, "stupid things," like unnecessary pharmacological or surgical intervention, can occur unless a reliable, principled doctor can be found to clarify matters. Most pain and distress only becomes perceptible—and then only with a certain delayed reaction—once the patient has given up his or her defensive behavior patterns: in other words, once a person has stopped taking medication or using other means to dull his or her senses. On the other hand, it is pointless to want to endure pain unnecessarily. Therapy, working as it does over an extended period of time, offers no shortcuts to resolving or alleviating pain, and a patient must decide how much he or she can bear.

The description of the therapy shows how unsatisfied needs can be transformed and how a healthy, integrated organism can replace a damaged one. If we are blind to our suffering, we will always try to sidestep our natural needs. As soon as we stop doing that, we encounter fear and pain. Therapeutic behavior enables us to resolve these by allowing our natural needs to assert their rights. Fear and pain, the Rosencrantz and Guildenstern of our existence, were originally intended by Nature as aids, and they will disappear as soon as we recognize and accept our own natural needs. Meanwhile, alarm signals in the form of fear and pain are only to be expected because our organism still regards our natural needs as dangerous, and we have no choice but to keep denying them. If we can understand this mechanism, it will help us in the therapeutic process. In certain cases, persons undergoing therapy may, for a short time, even feel worse, although objectively they are actually on the road to recovery. The reason for this is that at the same time that they are acknowledging their needs, they also anticipate punishment for doing so. This gives rise to feelings of fear and pain, particularly when they are called upon to truly defend themselves for once.

The strongest resistance to therapy—or, to put it more accurately, to the truth about one's own life and suffering—comes from the stubborn, relentless, and unfounded guilt feelings we have in us. Unreal feelings of guilt stem from situations in our past in which we were unable to adjust sufficiently or find a better solution. They come from emergency situations at a time in our lives when we were neither responsible for what was done to us nor capable of acting other than we did.

Parents constantly ask the question: how can I, as a mother or father, live with the knowledge not only that I was the victim of my parents and their way of bringing me up but that I did the same to my own children?

The answer isn't easy—or is it? For as long as we didn't know what was legitimate or right, how could we behave as we would have if we had not been injured in our primal integrity? Tragically, that applies to the way that we then behave toward our *own* children. With them we are least afraid of acting out our aggressions and insecurities. At the same time, it is above all with them that we want things to work out. Often it is our own children who are most directly exposed to, and affected by, our latent reactions and opinions. *Because we were blind we blindly handed suffering on to the next generation.*

In therapy, we ought to become more conscious not only of our rights as children but also of our duties as parents. When we encroach on our children's rights, we should immediately apologize and assure them that our irrational behavior was the product of our own problems and has nothing to do with them as people.

During the course of therapy, mistakes we made in the past will gradually become easier to recognize. The realization, however, will thereby become no less painful. For the moment, we can make our apologies to the child *in the therapy*—in so doing we have to practice all four steps of the method. In other words, we also have to acknowledge our confusion in the face of our life history and the way we transfer that to others. We have to formulate our insight into our wrongdoing and show our determination to act more justly. It is not always easy to have to admit how nasty and unpleasant one has been up to now, to have to realize how little that was positive or good resided in our souls and that we now have to get rid of the "junk" we have been saddled with if we are to at last live in accordance with our primal "I." "I" want to give and take only what is good and loving.

A Staff Member Reports

One thing that struck me as I read the letters we received after the appearance of the first two editions of this book was that many people obviously think that helping themselves could be dangerous.

Every symptom, fear, or pain demands from us that we stop for a moment and become conscious of what we are doing and why we are doing it. Reviewing one's immediate actions and behavior in the four steps of the therapy is a life-saving process. It can *never* be dangerous. Children who were once traumatized and unloved, tormented and made to feel insecure, find it difficult to differentiate between what is good for them and what is not, what is dangerous and what is helpful. So it does not surprise me that you have your doubts about what is essentially a simple, logical means of self-help in the four steps described by J. Konrad Stettbacher. How can one expect you to "take the plunge," trusting that everything will be okay, when you were so often confused as children? On the other hand, I am not surprised that you are so eager to place yourselves in good hands, helping hands that you have never known before. I know that this is a vital experience without which a child has no positive orientation and without which an adult is almost lost. Not only are we skeptical that such a thing exists. We also lack the positive experience we might use as a model. Our lack of orientation has impaired our ability to feel, sense, and think. At least a little of the feeling of knowing that one is being helped, that one is worth it and in the long term can help oneself, can be gained in therapy, given a good pair of helping hands. Naturally, it is much more difficult if one is forced to give oneself a helping hand, as it were, and undergo the therapy alone. But it is not impossible. It can be exhausting to be solely responsible for helping oneself. In this situation, if your energy resources are low and your living conditions bad, it is almost a hopeless endeavor—unless you adopt the attitude of "all or nothing."

The child you were would have welcomed this help. So help the child in yourselves as though it were your own dear one. Allow it time to develop and praise it for every step it takes. Give yourselves encouragement. What you are doing is a great achievement not only for yourselves but for everyone. As you now begin to work on your own life history, respect your feelings and try to understand them, even if they frighten you. They exist for a reason. Only alienated feelings can make you afraid. *I only* want to be good. *I* want *only* to love. If *I* am *compelled* to hate, I do not do it intentionally, and perhaps it is directed against the wrong person. Feelings of hate and rage that are not appropriate to the immediate situation make us ill. The child in you will reward you for the patience and care you devote to him, especially if you no longer allow him to suffer by mistreating yourself. One day you will be able to protect yourself, as far as possible, on your own and prevent anything from happening that is not good for you or for others.

My own experience has shown me that it is indeed possible to completely restore one's psychic integrity. Even physical injuries can be at least partially healed with time, though the scars will never completely disappear.

Appendix A

Hamburg, March 30, 1991

Dear Mr. Stettbacher, dear colleagues,

Today is Easter Monday, and I am at last in a position to report to you with joy that I am now as good as sure: I actually have been able to free myself from my recurring fears and pains (and also other irritating symptoms) with the help of your therapy which you describe in your book *Making Sense of Suffering.*

The decisive point in time was the day before yesterday, when I had the feeling, following an extensive "written therapy," that I had completed the "birth." It was a good and quite peaceful feeling.

I have been working alone with the therapy for more than five months and try to stick to your description as precisely as possible. To start with, I was full of enthusiasm and thought, "Give myself up? Never!" Later there were moments when doubts came whether I could succeed alone in picking up the thread again. But in the meantime, I have so much strength that I have tried it again and again. Basically, I had no alternative.

A precious help came from the For Your Information chapter, as these contributions again and again gave me the courage not to give up ("I shall succeed!").

I thank you very much for the clear description of your concept, with the help of which I can orient myself again and again. In fact, I have the feeling of getting the orientation (which I have been missing for so long) for the first time in my life—and I am 29 years old.

One question has been concerning me from the beginning: whether and how my own (caesarean section) birth has traumatized me. You personally do not deal specifically with caesarean section, but only with so-called difficult births. I would be interested to know whether you have experience with the consequences which caesarean section births generally can have for a child. Perhaps you will also receive other questions from other readers. My suggestion would be dealing with these questions in an additional chapter in a new edition.

I wish you and your colleagues all success and remain,

Yours sincerely,
Kathrin

Many similar letters have shown the efficiency of therapy without the immediate help of a therapist.

Appendix B

Why Are We So "Bad"?

Again and again, we are confronted with the question, why are we so "bad," so "evil"? By "bad" and "evil," I mean asocial, destructive, egocentric actions, actions that are hostile to life and indicate limited consciousness and lack of responsibility.

If we all were aware of the overall context in which we live, and if we were aware of our individual responsibilities in this world, we would not be "bad." But this capacity—for seeing and accepting responsibility—has not yet "grown" on a global basis. I have attempted to show why this is so in my book, *Making Sense of Suffering.*

The reason is injury done to each individual's primal integrity. These injuries occur as a result of negligence and primitive, unconscious emotional reactions.

They occur as often as they do because they often go unpunished. More powerful forms of life can afford to interfere aggressively with weaker or inferior beings without detriment to themselves. Man can and does act this way because, thanks to his enlarged brain, he has been able to create an array of "tools" and instruments of power that allow him to attack and exploit other forms of life—and by denying the destructiveness of his acts, to deceive those more vulnerable forms of life, as well as himself. Capricious interventions of this sort, which go unpunished in the short or long term, have increased in proportion to the loosening of the bonds that hold society together and to the diminishing of our dependency on our given, physical nature. The larger our scope of action and our seeming independence, the more we have been able to indulge our deception of both ourselves and other forms of life and evade our direct individual responsibilities. As a result, destructiveness has become more common, and suffering and injury to the fabric of life are becoming ever greater and more threatening, for all living things.

—J. Konrad Stettbacher, 1991

Appendix C

Caesarean Section

Births by caesarean section also belong in the category of "problem births," since children born by caesarean section are traumatized in very specific ways. Both bodily sensation, and the sense of achievement gained from one's own part in the act of birth, remains unknown to them. They are literally dragged screaming into the world. They are abruptly "brought to life—" pinched, slapped, and "reanimated." Because children delivered by caesarean section have to have the umbilical cord cut immediately after birth, a fear of suffocation and a burning feeling in the lungs can often remain as a persistent, if barely noticeable, threat for the rest of their lives.

The dread (unconscious fear) of "the human monster" is usually inherent in these children. The experience of being welcomed into the world, lying close to one's mother, and being lovingly cared for by her, with all the attendant feelings of bonding that this reawakens, is absent for the child born by caesarean section. A child who has been born in this manner and who is—as usually occurs—promptly separated from its mother after birth will retain the memory of this experience, like a birthmark on its consciousness. This memory will have a decisive significance for the rest of the child's life. Sequentially arranged, it looks like this:

1. Desire 2. Satisfaction 3. Stimulation 4. Shock (Anger) 5. Torture 6. Agony 7. Ruination.

On the other hand, the guiding principle of a psychically well person, one born in favorable circumstances, would look like this:

1. Desire
2. Satisfaction
3. Stimulation
4. Shock
5. Bodily Sensation
6. A Sense of Achievement from Individual, and Shared, Activity
7. Exhaustion
8. The Body Reunited With the Mother
9. Breathing Through One's Own Inhalation and Exhalation
10. A Sense of Security and Welcome With The Mother
11. Well-Being (*see* The Circuit, page 30.)

In the child, the following nexus establishes itself as a guiding principle: Desire–Joy–Stimulation–Shock (Anger), produces torture, agony, and ruination.

With children born by caesarean section, this guiding principle manifests itself differently than in those who experienced "normal births." The child's latent fear of being alone in this phase of its life will be commensurately great, in keeping with the leitmotifs of its birth: careless handling, abandonment, exposure to a hostile environment. This guiding principle operates in the case of every other "normal birth," that is, in births where the newborn in carelessly handled and its umbilical cord abruptly cut.

Watching films about caesarean section as a way of consciousness-raising can be a valuable aid to therapy. Universities generally have such films, which you can watch, with accompaniment if necessary.

Index